AF305164

BIG
TIME

ALSO BY LAURA VANDERKAM

168 Hours

All the Money in the World

What the Most Successful People Do Before Breakfast

I Know How She Does It

Off the Clock

Juliet's School of Possibilities

The New Corner Office

Tranquility by Tuesday

BIG
TIME

A Simple Path to Time Abundance

LAURA VANDERKAM

W. W. NORTON & COMPANY

Independent Publishers Since 1923

For information about permission to reproduce selections from this book, write to Permissions, W. W. Norton & Company, Inc., 500 Fifth Avenue, New York, NY 10110

For information about special discounts for bulk purchases, please contact W. W. Norton Special Sales at specialsales@wwnorton.com or 800-233-4830

Manufacturing by Lakeside Book Company
Book design by Daniel Lagin
Production manager: Julia Druskin

Library of Congress Cataloging-in-Publication Data Is available.

ISBN 978-1-324-11075-0

W. W. Norton & Company, Inc., 500 Fifth Avenue, New York, NY 10110
www.wwnorton.com

W. W. Norton & Company Ltd., 15 Carlisle Street, London W1D 3BS

Authorized EU representative: EAS, Mustamäe tee 50, 10621 Tallinn, Estonia

10 9 8 7 6 5 4 3 2 1

To my family

CONTENTS

BIG
TIME

HOW TO FALL IN LOVE WITH YOUR SCHEDULE

Time management, as a topic, does not inspire universal affection. How do you manage seconds slipping like sand through an hourglass? Time keeps moving forward, no matter what you want, and the general sense is that there's too much to do and too little time to do it in. We believe this on an immediate scale—"Why you'll never finish your to-do list" is a popular topic for productivity writers—and on a larger scale, as people lament decades flying past. We also bemoan the futility of it all. Time management implies control over time, but life does not go according to plan. For instance, I blocked out an hour from 4:00 to 5:00 p.m. to edit these next few paragraphs, and here it is, 5:12 p.m., because a series of alarms went off in my house, requiring me to ascertain whether we needed to evacuate immediately or if something sensitive just got damp.

So that is one way to view time. But it is not the only way.

Here is another. Let's imagine, for a moment, that you discover you are holding a winning lottery ticket. You're not quite sure why; you haven't been visiting the 7-Eleven daily hoping this would happen. You didn't even ask to play. The ticket was just handed to you, and now, improbably, you have a pot of cash to manage. You could complain that the prize should have been bigger. You could complain that you have to pay some amount of taxes. But I hope your general mood would be one of excitement—perhaps a heady sense of possibility.

When it comes to time, I think there's merit to this second approach. After all, the fact that any of us are even here to manage time is mind-boggling—including that we have conscious minds to be boggled. One of my random obsessions (and I'll admit, I have several) is the history of life on Earth, and particularly a catastrophe formally known as the Permian-Triassic extinction event. Approximately 252 million years ago, some 186 million years before the more famous asteroid took out the dinosaurs, a series of eruptions, climate shifts, and changes in oxygen levels eliminated 90 percent of the species on Earth. We live on such an improbable planet as it is, full of life when so much in our galactic neighborhood is not, and yet things could have ended right there.

They didn't, thankfully. But here's another thought to ponder if you find yourself awake in the middle of the night. If the terrible conditions of the late Permian had been terrible in just a *slightly different way*, perhaps a different set of species might have survived the great dying. Maybe the dinosaurs wouldn't have had their reign. Maybe there wouldn't have eventually been tiny mammals that later survived the asteroid hit. Maybe there wouldn't be primates. Maybe a species of them wouldn't have learned to walk upright, use fire, or read time-management books.

None of us has any business being here. That's true collectively, but also individually. With a slightly different set of historical events, or even a change in the precise moment of anyone's conception, you would not exist as *you*. And yet here you are. And here I am too. Given how improbable each minute of actually existing is, I prefer to view the hours as not somehow fewer than one hoped there would be, but all as being a bit of a bonus.

As for the futility of managing time given the unknowable future, it is true that nothing in life or the universe is ever really predictable in the long term. We never know how one thing will lead to another, how our lives will unfold, or that eruptions in Siberia 252 million years ago would lead, eventually, to a moment when one random human being would be writing these paragraphs.

And yet alongside that twisted path, there is a second truth. It is perhaps paradoxical, but one that is as sure as the unknowable future: We have an incredible amount of agency over the daily experience of our time. For instance, I recently went on a lovely early spring hike with a friend, where we discussed the Earth's post-Permian recovery during the Triassic, because, as mentioned, I'm kind of obsessed with the topic. That hike happened because I wanted to see my friend. So I texted her, and we both made space on a Friday afternoon and turned what could have been a forgettable hour on this improbable rock into something more pleasant.

The long run may always be uncertain, but we can shape our lives. It is by holding these two truths in mind simultaneously that we can become wise stewards of however many hours we happen to be able to direct—and over the course of a life, or even over the next year, I'll argue in this book, we'll probably be able to direct a lot.

This is why I find time management so magical. We've been given this amazing, unlikely resource—and we get to choose what to do with it! I know many people have an adversarial relationship with time. Our metaphors do violence as we aim to beat the clock, or at least race against it. We believe time is scarce, and comparing a human lifespan to geological time, of course that's true. But it would be true if people lived for centuries. Our own lives are all we know, and I'd argue that while life is finite, the daily experience of life is actually quite spacious. Almost everyone has some discretionary time, and many of us have a great deal if we're willing to be more organized and honest about it. There is reasonable evidence that we are *not* increasingly overworked or increasingly sleep deprived, or all the other alarming conjectures that make headlines. If I'd believed that time was scarce, I might not have tried to arrange a hike in the space of time as the work week was ending, and before my friend and I collected our various children. But when all time feels like it's a bit of a bonus, we can have a different mindset, and we can ask what we'd like to do with it.

This book is about what happens when you take the second perspective. What happens when you truly believe that time is abundant? What happens when you believe that time is big enough for you to create a life where you make a difference in your chosen field, enjoy meaningful relationships, pursue passion projects, have little adventures, and get open space too? What if you believe the trade-offs people lament are often illusions? What happens when you are mindful and intentional with the many hours that you can direct?

I believe that by adopting a more abundant perspective, even if we have a lot going on—perhaps *because* we have a lot going on—we can develop real affection for whatever time we get to experience.

This book is about how to fall in love with your schedule. It is about how to arrange your days on this improbable planet so you wake up knowing you have something to look forward to. Life may be finite, full of heartbreaks and setbacks, but time can be a friend for the journey. Over days and weeks and years, time in all its bigness can help you achieve things that would be impossible to do immediately.

I suppose at this point in the introduction, I should back up and introduce myself beyond my prehistoric obsessions. I've been writing about and studying time not quite since the Permian, but for about two decades now. I came to this topic when I stumbled upon the American Time Use Survey, and various historical time diary studies, and realized that many common perceptions about how people spend time, now and in the past, are wrong. I began collecting time diary data, from my own life and eventually from thousands of other people. I've written about my findings in a series of books on everything from morning routines to how successful women spend their time. I explore these topics in speeches, on my podcasts, in my newsletters, and so forth. I've been privileged to study thousands of people's schedules, and to have had conversations with people in all stages of life about how they shape their hours. I've experimented with the strategies I've learned in my own life as I've been managing my business, raising five children, and generally trying to keep this circus going.

Through this journey, I've kept coming back to a few ideas and images, and new ways of seeing time. In their own way, they've each become a little obsession alongside the extinction of the trilobites. I've looked for ways to write about them individually, but I eventually realized that they all had the common thread of moving beyond an adversarial relationship with time.

So in this book, I'm pulling them all together. This book explores many ways to fall in love with your schedule.

For instance, you can rewrite your story. When you audit your schedule and learn where the time really goes, you'll find that time is probably not as scarce as you think it is.

You can become the ringmaster. A complex circus of a life can be artfully managed with the right tools and the right mindset.

You can dream big but plan small. Over a long-enough period of time, you can do just about anything if you break the process into small-enough steps, and knowing you can do just about anything can make time feel surprisingly vast.

You can stop wishing time away. Even a boring workday can be made better with a few simple strategies.

You can embrace what I call your "golden hours," the weekday evenings that many struggle to enjoy intentionally. Time-management masters make the most of moments other people write off.

You can be open to serendipity. There are practical ways to create a life where wonderful opportunities seem to magically find you.

You can think in terms of the 8,760 hours in a year, and not the 24 hours in a day. Most trade-offs become less fraught when you view time from a bigger perspective.

You can also be patient. Happiness comes from being certain of the outcome while knowing that time is big enough for you to hold the timeline lightly.

To round things out, I include a Tactics section, with more detailed advice on implementing the ideas in this book, and a case study showing how one woman put all this advice together to embark on the path to time abundance.

I believe we can benefit from viewing time less as a foe and more as a friendly companion, present in enough quantities to be appreciated and savored. It might even be a more effective approach. People claim that time is scarce, but the sheer volume of time spent looking at social media ads suggests that we don't really believe time is precious. Maybe if we had a more abundant perspective we would stop hoping the minutes of a boring drive would move faster. We might see that this is real time and real space and perhaps listen to a beautiful Bach cantata to honor its spaciousness.

I know there is a lot of productivity advice in this world. Writing a book for busy people means asking busy people to spend at least a few hours of their lives reading when they could be doing other things such as, I don't know, pondering the end-Permian extinction. So I want to promise a few things to make the next few hours worth your while.

First, this book will be practical. My goal is for you to take lots of notes. I want you to come away with several ideas you are excited to try over the next few days. I want you to see how these strategies can help you enjoy your schedule and hopefully make the next year—the next 8,760 hours—the best of your life.

Second, this book will be new. In addition to stories and tactics, I share the results of several new time projects involving hundreds of people. I show what these men and women in all different stages of life and in diverse professions learned from tracking time and from trying my strategies in their daily lives. Even if you've read a lot of productivity books, including my books, you will find yourself saying "I never thought of it that way before."

And finally, I aim to be entertaining. Time can be a lens for looking at just about anything, from random prehistoric obsessions to the fascinating people sharing the planet with us.

Schedules might sound mundane, but how we spend our time is how we live our lives. I want everyone to fall in love with how they're spending their days, feeling that giddiness that one might feel at the beginning of any love affair. What marvelous thing will happen next? Making smart choices with our time can enable that, which is why I am so excited about this topic. I hope you will come to feel that way too.

Perhaps time is just an illusion— something people will occasionally announce to me in an attempt to shake up a random corporate workshop Q&A. It is true that weeks and hours are human constructs, but here's a fun fact: Back in the Mesozoic, a day was the equivalent of about 23 hours, and a bit over a billion years ago a day was about 19 hours. If you want an extra hour in the day, just stick around another 200 million years, as it turns out even natural time isn't as set as we might think.

But given all that, isn't it wonderful that we all can share this illusion and harness its power to make our daily lives better? I believe time is a gift, and it is big enough that we can create wonderful if improbable days.

This book is about how to do just that.

CHAPTER 1

REWRITE YOUR STORY

Joel Thomas is used to the comments by now. "You guys have so much going on!" or that exclamation, "I don't know how you do it." Joel is a school counselor, and his wife, Brittany, is a physical education teacher. They are raising four middle and elementary school aged kids in southwest Washington State. (Plus the occasional exchange student: "We're already busy with everyone else's stuff—what's one more kid?") The children practice martial arts, play soccer and baseball, and take dance classes. The family is involved in their church. They spend time with their extended family.

It is the usual mix of things—combined with not terribly flexible jobs—that can lead folks to a story of having no time. Day-to-day life certainly keeps Joel moving. He sent me a recent time log for a week showing 11 hours and 55 minutes spent on housework, 5 hours and 15 minutes spent on food prep, and three hours spent on errands, in addition to another 5-plus hours spent driving himself and various kids around. Add in the 5 hours he spent eating with his family, plus 4 hours of physical childcare (e.g., helping with bathing and dressing), plus the full-time job, and a lot of Joel's time is spoken for. The unpredictable becomes the predictable. He apologized for sending me his schedule later than he planned, but the kids' schools had been closed for several days due to snow.

One could forgive him for feeling like time is stretched.

And there have been moments that Joel has felt that way. But in the past few years, he decided that this story of scarcity is not particularly useful. Brittany's sister died in 2018 at age 35. Joel had lost his mother years ago, but when his father died shortly after his sister-in-law, it provoked a realization: "We're not guaranteed the time of the next day."

Time is precious, but, paradoxically, honoring that truth means recognizing that time can accommodate some rather hefty undertakings if you're mindful about how you use it. As Joel says, "When we get the sense that time is finite, it starts to put the focus on what is important." What would happen if he decided that time was big enough that he could do the things he wanted in life, alongside his obligations? What memories did he want to make? He had a lot of ideas, and he started to think about options.

For Joel, in addition to taking meaningful family trips (the crew once followed the footsteps of Brittany's World War II vet grandfather through Guam), he decided that meant trying to achieve his athletic goals without impacting family life. He'd long been fascinated by longer races. Not only did he want to regularly train for half-marathons and marathons, he also wanted to make space for the occasional ultramarathon (more than 26.2 miles).

So he looked at his time—all the 168 hours in a week. He tracked his time for several weeks over the years. He looked at when he needed to work, when he could usually be with his kids, and how much he needed to sleep. He saw what hours were available amid the food prep and housework, and the time Brittany wanted to devote to her own athletic goals.

The answer? A lot more time than you might think, if he was willing to move things around. Time is a limited resource, so "the time has to come from somewhere," he noted. But even in a busy life, it turns out that there are a reasonable number of "somewheres." Joel and Brittany figured out that if the couple skipped nightly television and went to sleep by 9:00 or 9:30 p.m., one of them could be up and exercising around 5:00 a.m. most mornings. They traded off the mornings when they had little ones, then eventually enjoyed the time dividend of their older kids being able to stay with sleeping younger siblings. Ninety minutes is enough to run 9 to 10 miles on an average morning. Do that a few times a week and the miles add up. Joel studied his time and saw that he used to spend a lot of time consuming news in the mornings. That could go too, giving him time to exercise *and* to interact with his family over breakfast. On weekends they would simply count back before Saturday soccer games or Sunday church, and whoever was headed out for a long run could time things to be back before then. A 5:30 to 8:30 a.m. shift can give you 20 miles before breakfast. A little longer gives you longer.

The result: Joel ran a 50-mile race in 2021. He participated in the Hood to Coast relay three times (a 200-mile venture, shared with friends). In November 2023 he logged his third 50K race (about 31 miles), and then in December he and Brittany ran the San Antonio Marathon together. When we talked again in early 2025, the couple had just run a half-marathon in Las Vegas with their older kids, and Joel had won a spot in the lottery for another 50-mile race that he had started training for, carefully plotting 4-hour runs into his schedule. He'd done all this while both he and Brittany were putting in five days a week at their workplaces, when they'd been covering the snow days, and he'd been logging those 11 hours and 55 minutes of housework necessary each week to keep the Thomas household functioning.

When Joel recounts all this running around to colleagues

and neighbors, sometimes they marvel. *How do you find the time?* But "I haven't really missed much that was happening," Joel says. Sometimes people talk about various shows he hasn't seen or sports teams he only casually follows. Perhaps he's a bit behind on the news. But "shifting my mindset from 'I don't have time' to 'It's not a priority' has been big," he says. "There really is a lot of time." Knowing where the time goes has let him change his story from one of a time crunch to one of possibility.

*　　　　　✳

YOU MAY HAVE NO INTEREST IN RUNNING 50 MILES. I DON'T. BUT perhaps there is something big in life that you would like to do. Perhaps you've been telling yourself that you'll get to it later, when things calm down, or that people like you simply don't have the space. How could you, with all you have going on? People have all kinds of stories they tell about time—about what is possible, about what normal people do, about what our commitments to others might still allow.

I hear these stories all the time as I speak with people about their schedules. I have met people juggling enough balls to put a circus clown to shame. But in this chapter I'm going to argue that, busy as we feel, most people are nowhere near the ceiling of what can happen in their lives. When we take a good look at how we are spending the hours we roll through, day by day, week by week, we find that a lot of the stories we tell of scarcity are not the whole picture. When we examine the data, a different picture emerges.

Life is probably not out of control. Free moments need not be snatched as mere ephemera. There is space for work, people, play, and more, if desired.

Perhaps that seems unlikely, but perhaps you can suspend your disbelief for the next few thousand words. Knowing where the time goes can help you rewrite your story from scarcity to abundance—and that, in turn, can make the next 8,760 hours the best of your life.

The storytelling impulse

Where does the time really go?

Despite the fact that we all experience time, all the time, and are possibly even obsessed with time (it is the most commonly used noun in the English language), this is a challenging question for most people to answer accurately. People have a rough sense of the last few hours. Thanks to various wearable devices, a growing number of people have some sense of time spent in bed. There might be a generally known rhythm to workdays—more so if time is billed or punched in and out for shifts—and an assumed rhythm to weekday evenings.

But though we tend to repeat our weekly schedules as the basic building blocks of our lives, many people don't know that there are 168 hours in a week or, for that matter, that there are 8,760 hours in a year. When we don't know the usual denominators for time, we are just guessing at the proportion of time devoted to things. A full-time job may feel like it takes the full amount of one's time. But 40 hours is less than 25 percent of 168 hours, and for someone sleeping 8 hours a night, it is approximately 36 percent of waking hours. And many people, even those who officially work full time, don't clock 40 hours every week. The average number of hours worked per year in the US has declined from about 2,300 in the 1920s to closer to 1,750 these days. Some people work more than others, of course, but it's hard to argue that the trend shows a society that is increasingly overworked, even if people claim that we are. As for other activities, according to the American Time Use Survey, in 2024 the average American spent 2.01 hours per day on "household activities" including cooking and cleaning, and 1.24 hours per day on eating and drinking, but I'd bet few people could guess those figures with any accuracy. Who knows what proportion of time is spent showering, or driving, or reading, or anything else?

It is not just proportions that are fuzzy. Once time has passed, it lingers only in impressions. Where did the time go on October 19, 2022, or January 26, 2018, or May 6, 2015, or any other day one could have a random date generator cough up? These days happened. If you were alive to experience them, the time went somewhere. Time is always spent on something. But as time disappears into the wash of history, it becomes even more subject to forgetfulness or memory's storytelling impulse.

I am as prone to those vagaries as anyone else, but I actually do know how I spent October 19, 2022, January 26, 2018, May 6, 2015, and all the other days of the past decade and change. I started tracking my time one week in April 2015, figuring the data might be useful. Then I just kept going. I use weekly spreadsheets that start at 5:00 a.m. Monday morning and, with the days of the week across the top and half hour blocks down the left-hand side, go to the following Monday at 4:30 a.m. These 336 cells represent the 168-hour week. I check in three times a day and write in rough detail ("work," "run on treadmill," "drive H to school") what I have done since the last check-in.

For instance, on Friday, January 26, 2018, I was having trouble sleeping in the hotel room outside Montreal, Canada, that I was sharing with my family. So in the 5:00 a.m. cell I wrote: "5:15 up, move to bathroom," where I guess I couldn't hear anyone snoring. The day was redeemed, though, as the kids and my husband went skiing and I (because I am terrified of skiing) squirreled myself away in the hotel to do a little work (9:45 to 10:15 a.m.), visit the hotel gym, enjoy a massage (12:00 to 1:00 p.m.), and then later take the kids to the outdoor hot tub

(4:15 to 4:45 p.m.), where we experienced the surreal sensation of having very warm bodies with snow falling on our very cold noses. The time entries are all there on the log, and so when I open any given week and look at it, the memories come back quickly enough.

As my time-tracking week goes Monday to Monday, every Monday morning I fill in the last few cells from the week, archive the log, and then open a new one.

Much of what fills these logs—more than 500 weeks and counting in my Excel "book of hours"—is mundane. But because I have recorded when I work, sleep, cook dinner, or take care of my kids, I know how much time I have spent on these things and regularly spend on these things. I know where my hours have gone. Since we live our lives in hours, I have a clear sense of what my life really looks like.

This matters for a simple reason. Most of us would like to spend our time well. As perfection is elusive, that tends to mean "better than I am spending my time now." But if you want to spend your time better, then you need to know where the time is going now—because if you don't, how will you know if you're changing the right thing? Maybe something you thought was a problem really isn't. Maybe something you didn't think of is taking more time than you imagined. Like any business decision, it helps to work from good data.

In the absence of data, we build stories based on the moments that register. Human nature being what it is, negative moments stand out more than the positive ones. From your spouse's withering glance when you snuck back to your home office for a 7:00 p.m. conference call the other night, you feel, vaguely, that you are working too much, but the exact amount is unclear. George, who was staffed on that last project with you, complains about his 60-hour workweeks and, come on, you *know* you're working more than George. By the time you were finished doing the dishes last night—it feels like you spend your life doing dishes!—there wasn't time to read that magazine before you were too tired to keep your eyes open. Time starts to feel scarce. You are too busy. Life is unsustainable. You know this to be true.

But do you? Why not try tracking your time for a week and see what it looks like?

Sometimes people think this exercise is about playing "gotcha," and that my goal when I suggest people track their time for a week is to point out the two hours spent watching Netflix when someone feels like they're drowning. But honestly, I do not care about the streaming or scrolling, which everyone does. Even after a decade of tracking, I know I still waste time.

Instead, I want to promise something different—something that might help with the drowning. I now know that when I had a few hundred people track their time for a week, their time satisfaction levels as I measured them improved significantly during this time. Based on their responses, and on all the time logs sent to me over the years, I now believe that tracking your time makes you happier about your time. The truth sets us free, and knowing where the time goes lets us tell ourselves a different story about our lives—one in which we often *are* spending time on what matters and problems aren't existential. They are solvable with practical shifts in time allocation. Time is a resource to be used, much like silver in a mine, and there is more of it than you have probably imagined.

The Time Tracking Challenge

Most Januarys I run a weeklong project in which thousands of people sign up to track their time together. I send participants a time log and instructions. You can see more detailed instructions on how to track your time in the Tactics section at the end of the book, starting at page 172, but it's a fairly straightforward process:

Choose a week to track. You should also choose a method for tracking. I like my spreadsheets, but you can also use an app, or write notes in a journal.

Check in three or four times per day. Note what you've done since the last time you checked in. Some people like to use broad categories such as work, sleep, housework, family time, and leisure time, and some people like to be more descriptive or detailed. The former will make it easier to create a nifty pie chart, if that's something you care about, but the latter might give you more information to work with. This is a personal choice.

Try to keep going for a week. If you forget, just start back up again. It's okay if a few entries are blank.

Study the results. After a week, add up the major categories if you wish, or just ask what you like or don't like.

Over the years, many people have sent me their logs and their observations. I file away interesting testimonials, often from busy people who manage to manufacture even more time. A physician, for instance, once told me that life had felt out of control. Then she tracked her time for a week and saw on the spreadsheet that her work hours and other obligations looked quite reasonable as a proportion of the total canvas. Indeed, she had time to pick up an extra volunteer shift with an organization that inspired her and gave her more energy for everything else in life. "Time blindness is real," she told me. And an accountant who'd billed her work time in small increments for years still learned something by tracking the rest of her time—namely, that she had quite a bit of control over it. "The more I have control over my time, the more I'm actively choosing it, the less stressed I am," she said.

Anecdotes mean little on their own, though. So in January 2023, I decided to look into the effects of tracking time more systematically for what I began calling the "Time Tracking Challenge." I used a time-satisfaction scale that I have used for several projects over the years to measure how people feel about their time. On a scale of 1 to 7, with 1 being "strongly disagree" and 7 being "strongly agree," people would state how they felt about the following statements.

- Yesterday, I had enough time for the things I wanted to do.
- Yesterday, I got enough sleep to feel well rested.
- Yesterday, I made progress on my professional goals.
- Yesterday, I made progress on my personal goals.
- Yesterday, I had enough energy to handle my responsibilities.
- Yesterday, I was happy with how I spent my leisure time.
- Yesterday, I did not waste time on things that weren't important to me.
- Generally, I have enough time for the things I want to do.
- Generally, I have the energy for the things I want to do.
- Overall, I feel good about my relationships and my progress on my personal priorities.
- Overall, I'm making progress on my professional goals.
- Generally, how I spend my time aligns with my priorities and my values.
- I regularly have time just for me.

The first seven statements are designed to measure people's satisfaction with a particular day (i.e., yesterday), with the last six looking at how people generally feel.

I asked people who signed up for my January 2023 Time Tracking Challenge to fill out a pre-challenge survey to establish a baseline level of time satisfaction. I asked several open-ended questions to learn about people's attitudes toward time. I then asked people to fill out a second survey after they'd tracked time for a week.

As with any project, not everyone filled out the surveys. You may not be surprised to learn that people who completed the post-challenge survey had higher initial time satisfaction scores than people who did not fill out the final survey. Perhaps people who were able to stick with time tracking for a week—or at least complete both surveys—felt happier with their time and less overwhelmed than people who didn't complete the second survey. So to have usable results, I looked only at the 279 people who filled out both surveys within a day or two of receiving them.

However, even within this smaller group of conscientious folks, I saw statistically significant increases in time satisfaction for both the "yesterday" subscale and the "generally" subscale. Given all the feedback I've received about time tracking over the years, I wasn't surprised to see that scores rose. However, what I found most intriguing is that the "generally" scores rose more than the "yesterday" scores.

An increase in a "yesterday" score seems straightforward. Time tracking provides accountability. Most people don't want to document a three-hour YouTube binge on their time logs, so they choose to do more fulfilling things. Then they feel better about the day.

An attitude shift about time "generally," on the other hand, suggests something else is going on.

It could be that, after a week of making better choices "yesterday," people start to see themselves as the kind of people who make better choices overall.

But it may also be that people who track their time realize that life isn't as frenzied or crunched as they may have been imagining. Life certainly isn't perfect, but time is big enough for us to do what matters. From studying people's open-ended answers, I think the latter is the more powerful explanation.

What the data show

My 279 time trackers began that January week with a reasonable relationship with time (a 4.55 average on the 1-to-7-point scale for the 13 statements). Even so, many people's initial time stories conveyed that background noise of scarcity:

> "I never quite get to the things I really want to do."

> "I have been 'battling' with time and time management for a while."

> "My job can be all-consuming. I need better boundaries."

> "I am not feeling in control of my time but rather reactive to every deadline, meeting, and personal event, which results in frantic, last-minute prep."

> "I know I'm not using all of my time wisely and always wish I had more time in a day."

> "My mindset of time poverty is cutting through opportunities to build meaning and social connection in my life."

> "I want to stop viewing time and my to-do list as a heavy weight."

I know these feelings are common, particularly among productive people. We have a lot going on. We are managing many things. We work hard to meet expectations. All this can generate stress of the sort that makes any given incident, like being three minutes late to an important meeting, feel like evidence that life is out of control.

My time trackers logged their time for a week from 5:00 a.m. Monday, January 9, to 4:30 a.m. Monday, January 16. Along the way, I suggested they look at their hours and add up categories of interest, note what they liked most about their time, and think about what they'd like to spend more time doing and less time doing.

As they analyzed their time, people did find moments they weren't thrilled with.

One woman wrote that it was "pretty galling to have to write, 'watched YouTube with my husband' every night after the kids went to bed." Someone else noted what they considered an excessive amount of time spent playing a video game. Someone realized that they spent far too much time getting ready, and wasted time between activities. Another noted an eye-opening amount of time spent hitting the snooze button. One person realized that "I go into the weekend without a plan for what to do and fritter away the time." Another lamented a work schedule filled with meetings to advance everyone's goals except their own.

Happily, seeing specific problems nudged people to think about solutions. A person who reported spending "an embarrassing amount of time at work on 'admin items'" decided to block out time for administrative work to leave other time open for bigger projects. Someone who observed that she became more distracted at work as she got tired decided to proactively plan breaks. Many noted that tracking made them more mindful of making better choices in the moment—the experience that results in higher "yesterday" scores.

"I saw some habits that I knew I needed to work on but were highlighted in a more obvious way," one person wrote. "It allowed me to start thinking about how to change that behavior."

As people made these choices, agreement with the seven "yesterday" statements rose 12 percent over the course of the week. Agreement with the statement "Yesterday, I did not waste time on things that weren't important to me" rose 19 percent over the course of the week. "Now I ask myself more frequently mid-activity: Is this worth my time?" one person noted.

These yesterday scores showed a significant rise, but the "generally" subscale scores rose even more, by 18 percent over the week. Agreement with the hopeful statement "Generally I have enough time for the things I want to do," rose 25 percent.

This is a big change over the course of seven days. Some of the 279 time trackers saw this as a life-shifting increase. In the open-ended responses I could see that people's stories were changing. Their sense of time was shifting from it being scarce to it being more abundant than they realized.

Often this happened because the data showed that their impressions about their lives were incomplete. Working long hours, or longer than you hoped to on a particular day, doesn't mean you are working around the clock. One bad night being up with a toddler and then catching an early plane doesn't mean you never sleep. Needing to empty the dishwasher and help a child with homework doesn't mean you never have time for yourself. Logging time showed people that work, family and household responsibilities, and sleep didn't fill all the hours in the grids on their spreadsheets. Time must be spent on something. Sometimes those other hours were spent well and sometimes they were not, but most important, they were *there*. One hundred sixty-eight hours is a vast amount of time.

As they analyzed their hours, people realized all sorts of things. For instance, work and housework hours are often more prominent in the narrative than in reality:

"I estimated I would work 60 to 70 hours and worked 53.5."

"I'm supposed to work 40 hours a week (salaried), but I only logged 31.75 . . . it wasn't a completely typical workweek as far as tasks go, but I am spending less time doing work than I realize."

"I discovered activities that it seems take longer (unloading the dishwasher) are extremely quick and probably total 15 minutes all week even if I am the one doing it each day."

People were also surprised to see how much discretionary time they had:

"I get *way* more time to myself than I thought I did."

"There were several things that I did three times a week (creative pursuits mostly) that I felt like I didn't ever do because I didn't do them daily."

"I am a single mom of two [who] works full-time outside the home. I love to read and feel like I don't have time to. But from tracking my time, I am learning that I have pockets of time that I do get to do what I want to do."

Many working parents were amazed at how much time they were still clocking with their kids:

"Family time is important to me, but I wasn't sure it would be reflected in how I actually spent my time. I was happy to see how high that percentage turned out to be."

Indeed, some people began to see that the trade-offs they'd been assuming life required weren't necessary, because there was so much more space than they thought.

One person who'd had a habit of doing a little work at night—and then seeing this bleed into half working and half watching Netflix when she got tired—decided to consciously stop spending her hours in this unproductive way. She started using the evenings to go to the gym or spend time with family, and felt more productive at work because she forced herself to be done by quitting time. "While it seems impossible, [time tracking] has already improved my ability to meet my personal and professional goals and to improve my relationships," she reported. "I didn't realize how much those 'working' hours in the evening were draining my energy while not really accomplishing much toward my goals until I realized I had to fill the time in on a log and deal with it." Another person realized that despite the general narrative of workdays being fragmented and distracted, there actually were large chunks of uninterrupted time for working on a key project. "The log gave me an opportunity to realize and appreciate that."

There's more time than you think

With all these epiphanies came increased time satisfaction. Agreement with the statement "Generally, how I spend my time aligns with my priorities and values" rose 13 percent. Agreement with the statement "I regularly have time just for me," rose 15 percent.

I believe that tracking your time will lead to increased time satisfaction for you too. As one time tracker said, "Tracking time takes away that treadmill feeling and gives a 30,000-foot view of your week."

Another person noted: "It's so incredibly helpful to actually see where you're spending your time. The only person looking/judging this is you—so how do you *want* to spend your time? There's way more time than you think."

This last statement is my philosophy for life. Even busy people do have some space. Some simply acknowledge this. There is time to relax, to savor, to breathe. People often wish for more margin in their lives. For the vast majority of people, figuring out where the time really goes will reveal that there is *already* some margin available if you choose to see it. Those 45 minutes spent doomscrolling at night could have been spent relaxing instead. That hour spent puttering around the house Saturday didn't accomplish anything, so it could have been spent lying on the grass looking up at the clouds if you'd like. When you do see this space, you see that there is a simple path to a sense of time abundance. Life is good.

But—and this brings us back to Joel Thomas with his ultramarathons—sometimes people decide that there is space for something more in life. They see this even amid family responsibilities and long or inflexible work hours.

Mike Ely, who tracked his time for a decade while he was starting a church as a missionary in Romania, said, "People kind of assume they have this ceiling, like 'my whole life is work.'" Time tracking showed Mike that even with the unpredictability of ministry, he had half of his time for other things. The new story became "Sure, I have this job and it feels like it consumes my life, but it's actually less than 50 percent of my waking hours. I have this canvas I can work with."

When you rewrite your story from one of scarcity to one of

abundance, you start to realize that what you thought were the limits on possibility may not be there. Maybe other people want to accept more restrictions and paint on a smaller part of their life's canvas. Maybe they want to shout about how small that canvas is or that no one can "have it all." But unless they have a good numerical sense of where all the time truly goes, they don't know that, possibly not for themselves and certainly not for you. When we take a more expansive view, we might surprise ourselves, and everyone around us, with what will comfortably fit into the next 8,760 hours.

That was the case for Viktorija Grant. Our paths crossed in December 2017, when I traveled to Chicago to give a speech at the company where she had recently started working.

Viktorija later told me that my talk came at a fortuitous time for her. She was hoping to earn a master of business administration degree, which she thought would open up new leadership opportunities for her. But she and her husband also felt called to start a family and didn't want to wait several years until she was done with school. So, the key question: Was it possible to do both at the same time? She had been thinking about this a lot, because when she looked around at the school where her husband was earning an MBA, she saw that "there were no mothers in my husband's program," or at least not ones with young children. She hunted through her broader network to see if anyone else had had babies during an MBA program, but her search came up empty. "I couldn't find anyone who could walk me through that journey," she said.

She later told me, "The two dreams seemed incompatible . . . until they weren't."

I'm not sure exactly what I said to light this spark of possibility, but the ember grew as she read stories in my books and in other places about people who decided time was big enough that they could build substantial careers while building their families.

She decided that if she took a good look at her hours, she might realize that she had enough time to make her various dreams come true. "I could look at my time as a resource that should be used thoughtfully and intentionally."

Excited by this possibility, she decided to do some research. Her first step was to figure out exactly how much time earning an MBA would take on a weekly basis. She tracked her husband's time, and she looked at other people in other programs, particularly those that catered to working professionals. She could track how much time she was working—something she planned to continue doing—and she could see how much time she wasn't working. Figuring out how much time a baby would require is obviously a different matter. "Being a mom is a twenty-four/seven job," as she noted, but she could also figure out when she could share care with her husband (in their "joint pool of hours"), and what daycare coverage would look like.

The math looked like it would work, as long as she cut some extraneous stuff from her life. "I canceled my Netflix account," she said. One thing led to another. She took the GMAT (Graduate Management Admission Test) in late September 2018 while six months pregnant. She began an MBA program at Northwestern's Kellogg School of Management with her baby daughter along for the ride.

The process was not easy by any means, but "it was actually quite manageable," she said. She took the majority of her classes on Saturdays when her husband had their daughter. Even though the work wouldn't be due until the following Saturday, she aimed to do as much of her homework on Sundays as she could—often during naps or after her daughter went to bed (the family became quite diligent about bedtimes). This idea of "shifting everything left"—as in, doing her work long before it needed to be done—paid off in many ways. If things went wrong, as can happen with a baby, she still had six days to finish her MBA work. Meanwhile, her careful attention to identifying what was most important, and then doing those things as far ahead of time as possible, led to her advancing at work as well. Soon, she was managing a team.

After two and a half years, she graduated with distinction from her MBA program while pregnant with her second daughter. As she noted, "Life is lived in hours," and when she paid attention to those hours, she was able to make more fit than she originally thought was possible. At alumni networking events, her classmates still refer to Viktorija as "the one who had the baby"—as if she had done something almost mystical. Except that it really wasn't. "I didn't feel like my hair was on fire," she said. She simply rewrote her story and spent her hours on what mattered to her, which has resulted in her continuing to grow her career into bigger management roles, continuing to grow her family (she welcomed a third child, a little boy, in 2024), and even finding time to study piano alongside her oldest child.

I love Viktorija's approach. If there is something you would like to do in life, maybe you can adopt the same mindset. Figure out where your time is going now. Figure out how much time your goal will take. Figure out how you might plot those hours into the existing space, leaving a buffer for what might go wrong. You might need to be creative, using mornings like Joel, sharing care with others like Viktorija, looking at the whole of your time rather than any individual day, and other time management strategies we'll discuss in this book. But I suspect that pretty soon you will be able to rewrite your story for what is possible—in any given week, and in the next 8,760 hours too.

"People think time is scarce, so they can't do anything, so they don't do anything," Mike Ely says. Flip that around, and time simply opens up.

CHAPTER 2

BECOME THE RINGMASTER

According to my time logs, on July 21, 2024, at exactly 3:29 p.m., I watched Alex Cortes get shot out of a cannon. Commander Alexander, as he is known onstage, was at the York State Fair in Pennsylvania as part of the Flying Cortes act, a traveling troupe of his extended family members who perform a variety of the circus arts. I'd gone to the fair with my family for a little weekend adventure. We sat to watch the three o'clock show, and marveled as the acrobats swung back and forth on the trapezes.

It was exciting, but we were wilting from the heat, and so we were headed somewhere indoors when a lady next to me said we might want to wait. The cannon act was next. Sure enough, Commander Alexander proceeded to climb down the shaft of a 28-foot-long gleaming white cannon. We counted down from 10, and as my husband videotaped the whole thing in slow motion, off Alex Cortes went, flying through the air at about 70 miles per hour, and landing, safely, on a giant mat.

Seeing someone fly through the summer sky is certainly memorable. I watched that video a great many times. And so, after I was back at my desk the next week, I reached out to Commander Alexander to see if he might chat about his job and the circus life in general.

He told me that while he's a lifelong trapeze artist—he began learning to do tricks not long after coming to the US from Colombia as a baby in 1977—he began the cannon phase of his career in 2023. A friend who did gigs as a human cannonball, and who built and sold circus cannons, had been on him to give it a shot.

The flying and, more critically, the landing part wasn't hard for a professional acrobat. "Once you're in the air, the body movements—well, you know how to control your body in the air," Commander Alexander told me. But he had to learn the meticulous art of how to work the cannon and how to angle it exactly right so that he would fly the right distance to the waiting mat. "There's a lot of math that goes into it," he said. As for his maiden voyages, "you shoot very short. You move up in small increments." After a lot of repetition, the act was ready.

Getting shot out of a cannon isn't comfortable. "It's hot in there!" he said. On a day like the one at the York State Fair, with temperatures in the 90s, he told me that it can reach above 120 degrees inside the cannon. He also deals with some nerves. "I have to inspect the cannon after every single shot," he said. "There's always questions—Did I check this? Did I check that?—that go through my mind." Every second of the act is carefully planned.

That's true for the trapeze sequence as well. Commander Alexander talked me through how the catcher (who is usually hanging upside down from his knees so his arms are free) beats out his swings back and forth. He adjusts based on how he sees the other performers move. For the more complicated tricks, four or more people have to do their designated movements to exact specifications, executing them within a fraction of a second.

Things can go wrong. That's why the trapeze apparatus is positioned over a net. To my thinking, a net was a net, but Commander Alexander quickly changed my mind. "The net takes a huge beating. We have to be on top of it all the time," he said. The Cortes family often performs outside, and even a well-practiced, simple stunt can go awry with a big gust of wind. No one wants to land in the net during a show—they fall from high enough that the net can bounce them 8 to 10 feet in the air—but it is inevitable, and better than the alternative. So they check the net and repair it frequently, and from the beginning, "we train ourselves to land in the net in a certain way."

That also means that the net has to be exactly where the performers expect it to be. If the Cortes family performs in an indoor circus where they need to change the height of their trapeze apparatus a bit, then "we have to adjust the nets to be the same height from us as with a normal apparatus," he told me. Even a few inches of difference might mean someone would overrotate and land in a way that could lead to injury or worse.

It sounds intense, but Commander Alexander, who told me he took a job building cubicles when circuses shut down during the COVID-19 pandemic, says there are plenty of upsides to this kind of life. Ultimately "it is a lot of fun," he said. Rather than sit in one of those cubicles, he gets shot out of a cannon two to three times on a performance day. "It definitely is a huge rush every time I go in there."

✳

"MY LIFE IS A CIRCUS!" I HEARD THAT COMPLAINT NOT LONG AGO from someone whose schedule was feeling out of control. You know how it goes. Nothing happens when it is supposed to. A series of errors leads to an accelerating sense of chaos.

I sympathized with the person complaining, but with the

human cannonball stunt fresh in my mind I had a different thought: Honey, you *wish* your life was a circus.

When the Flying Cortes family members take the stage, everyone knows exactly what they are supposed to do, and they go exactly where they are supposed to go at exactly the time they are supposed to be there. When things go wrong, everyone knows how to land in the net. The net is as tested and well positioned as anything else on the stage. Complexity appears seamless.

Indeed, in our quest to fall in love with our schedules, I believe we should consciously embrace this idea of life being a circus. Daily life is complex, but it can be orderly. Not only that, we should aim to be the ringmasters of our lives, calmly in charge of it all. Everything is well planned. Processes are strong. Mistakes are anticipated and prepared for, so everyone can keep moving forward even when they happen. Maybe it's not for everyone, but I believe that with a little smart strategy, creating a big and wonderful life can look as magnificent as a well-timed catch on a flying trapeze.

How to embrace the bigness

Every month for the last 20 years, my copy of *Real Simple* magazine has shown up in the mail. During this time, many of my other favorite magazines have ceased publishing. But this one keeps going. It seems we are drawn to that word "simple" (perhaps why I threw it in my subtitle!), or simplicity's cousin, minimalism, which has taken over social media. People salivate over Instagram posts of earth-toned nurseries devoid of actual toys.

Modern life can feel overwhelming. The idea of paring back appeals. Create more margin! Limit all commitments! Happiness is gained by pursuing less. I admit that I am intrigued by neutral design palettes, and the promise that an entire family can live calmly in a tiny house.

Appealing as it may be, though, my life is structurally complex. Having one child would be simpler than having five children. But I have five. So here we are.

I am far from the only one whose life features structural complexity. Any two-working-parent household, no matter how many kids are living in it, will involve a lot of moving parts. Solo parents have all sorts of schedule puzzles to figure out. Some people are caring for relatives with evolving medical conditions. Some people work multiple jobs. Some people's jobs, such as being a high school principal, will involve shifting schedules and keeping lots of people happy. You have to learn to live in this circus act.

And so people do, and in their managing, show that there is no need to simplify just to simplify. Complexity isn't the enemy. Chaos is. Complexity and chaos are not the same things at all. Indeed, certain kinds of joy are only possible if you choose the bigger life.

This chapter is about how to adopt this mindset of becoming the ringmaster of your own life, embracing the bigness that's part of a spectacular show. Managing three rings—your career, your relationships, and yourself—comes down to a few principles. First, everything is well planned (including a great many set processes that don't have to be planned over and over again). Next, there is a flexibility to everything—a good net, if you will—for when things go wrong. And finally, all this looks like magic, because no one enjoys a circus that looks like drudgery. A good ringmaster manages for delight.

1. Plan your circus

A few hundred miles west of the York State Fair, Kurt Cockran is also managing quite the circus. This Lutheran pastor and his wife have five children under the age of 10. He told me in an email that earlier in his ministry career, he felt "overwhelmed and over-loaded," that he was "not managing my time and tasks well, and not figuring out how to balance ministry and home life." While navigating a particularly conflict-ridden congregation, and dealing with the pressure of an increasing number of obligations and the need to respond to messages arriving at all hours, he told me that he wound up deeply depressed. It did not seem possible to enjoy a career where expectations exceeded the time available.

However, while transitioning to his next ministry, he decided to pour himself into productivity literature. The goal was to figure out how to better manage all the circus rings of work and his growing family.

In seminary he had heard a presentation on David Allen's book *Getting Things Done* and had implemented some organization systems with Excel, but "the biggest thing I lacked conviction on was weekly planning," he says. He decided to start planning his life more thoroughly, and eventually he came up with a few ways to keep the three rings going.

These days, he and his wife, Emily, have a sitter come for a couple of hours on Friday mornings while they walk the neighborhood, reflect on home life, brainstorm what improvements can be made, and plan the upcoming week. During the week, as ideas and new information come up, they use a shared Google Keep note titled "Docket of items to discuss," where they add topics to talk about in person instead of relying on back-and-forth messaging. As part of his planning, Kurt thinks of the week in terms of "21 pods"—a method he tells me has something of a cult following among pastors. The idea is that the main daytime hours of the seven days of the week are split into 3 pods of about four hours each (morning being roughly 8:00 a.m. to 12:00 p.m., afternoon 12:00 to 4:00, and evening 4:00 to 8:00, or perhaps a little later). Each week Kurt chooses 10 to 12 pods to be "work pods." This helps to ensure a sustainable 40- to 50-hour work-week, even if it is spread over a broader range of days and hours than a typical office job. He thinks through what needs to happen for his ministry work during this time.

As for managing family life, he and Emily maintain a giant weekly plan refrigerator magnet to keep track of upcoming obligations for everyone. Kurt aims to leave enough space for this ring of the circus by publicizing to the congregation when he will be off work, and when he is more available for appointments. While this is not foolproof (ministry has its emergencies), a well-functioning church like his current one generally has a system of coverage that limits how often a minister would be called during unexpected times. This allows Kurt to commit to things in his home life. He also limits how much work spills over into other pods by using the project-management tool Trello to keep track of what he's waiting to hear back on, so he doesn't need to ruminate about what he's forgetting. He schedules messages to go out at certain times, so responses tend to arrive during his work pods. This reduces the pressure to respond during a family or personal pod, as do his office hours (4:30 to 5:30 p.m. Wednesday and Friday), when anyone can reach him with "no notice needed."

During the Friday morning meeting, Kurt and Emily try to make it through anything that needs to be discussed. The goal is to figure out what is most important, and to have their marching orders in place for the week, so that they do not need to be constantly dealing with logistics the rest of the time.

Things do not go perfectly. But the upside of knowing who needs to be where and when is that when things don't go perfectly, solutions are fairly easy to figure out. For instance, on a day around the time I interviewed Kurt, he had finished a work pod and come home to find that Emily had experienced a rough afternoon with the kids. She hadn't had time to prepare for an online class she was teaching the next day. A child also had a baseball game. So rather than everyone going to the baseball game, they decided that Kurt would stay home with the four other kids, and Emily would go to the game with her laptop and prepare during those hours that the leisurely pace of children's baseball games created. Everything got done.

Depression and burnout are serious things. Weekly planning sessions, refrigerator magnets, and such might seem trivial in comparison. And yet, a few years into a new ministry in Indiana, Kurt reports that "my depression has gone away entirely." There is great power in deciding that life can be complex but not chaotic, and that managing the complexities is possible.

Kurt used to believe "that I could be an excellent pastor or an excellent father/husband, but it's not possible to be both. Or that I can be a mediocre husband/father and a mediocre pastor, but I can't expect to achieve excellence in either," he says. He has now discarded this belief and has decided that excellence in both spheres might be possible. He's even found time to join a recreational soccer league to make sure that third circus ring of personal pursuits exists. (Emily has a boxing setup in the garage where she gets her me-time.) He's been pondering, when the kids are older, writing his own productivity books—or perhaps starting an organization to help other overwhelmed pastors become the ringmasters of their lives.

I BELIEVE KURT IS ONTO SOMETHING WITH HIS SYSTEMATIC AP-proach. We won't all plan in the same way that Kurt does, with pods and the like, but a good ringmaster does have a solid sense of what is going on in his life in all three rings at all times. The only way to get that sense is to have a time, regularly, when you review what is happening, what needs to happen, and what you want to have happen.

Most of us live our lives in weeks, in the sense that this is the repeating pattern of when things happen in our lives. So a weekly planning session, for most people, is the best way to ensure a holistic sense of what's going on.

I do my weekly planning late in the week, just as Kurt does with Friday mornings. I think a Thursday or Friday slot is best for a few reasons.

You might not be doing much else. Most people run out of steam for tackling big projects by the end of the workweek, and so the opportunity cost of time later in the week is lower.

You can connect if you need to. Planning on Thursday or Friday during business hours (versus over the weekend) means that if you need to make an appointment or get a response from someone as you're planning, people are more likely to be available.

You'll feel less anxious. Knowing what you'll be doing Monday morning before you go into the weekend can combat the "Sunday Scaries," that vague sense of unease when you know you have a lot on your plate but don't know how you'll deal with it.

You get a chance to plan each weekend twice. You can look at the one coming up at the end of the next Monday to Sunday week and the one that's coming up immediately. That level of attention will lead to better weekends.

All that said, the specific time isn't critical. If you love your Sunday-evening or Monday-morning planning session, I'm not asking you to switch. What matters is that you, the ringmaster, have a regular time when you check in and figure out the next week's run of show.

Hopefully you have some sort of calendar where you keep track of your various commitments (there's more advice on how to make this system airtight in the Tactics section at the end of the book). During your weekly planning session, study your calendar, note what is on there, and the desires and obligations of others whose schedules might affect yours.

Then, once you've got a sense of the landscape, you can make yourself a priority list for the upcoming week. These days I do this on a page in a fancy planner, but for many years I used a cheap notebook from Target. The tool doesn't matter. What matters is the doing.

For most busy people, life is a circus with three main rings:

Career. This category encompasses anything relating to your professional life (or to your education if you're a student, or to your major volunteer work if that's a big part of your schedule).

Relationships. This category consists of priorities related to family and friends, and could also encompass the broader community.

Self. This category is for activities that contribute to your physical, mental, emotional, and spiritual health.

There will be overlapping areas, but these categories are reasonably comprehensive. So I suggest dividing your priority list for the upcoming week into these three categories. As a practical matter, I make the left column on my planner page my professional priority list, and the right column contains relationships and self. This works because, often, "self" will be on the smaller side. But it shouldn't be invisible. Don't leave the category blank. You can guarantee yourself a more balanced life by making sure there is something going on in all three rings.

Then, look over your calendar and start making your lists. What is happening in your professional life that is most important? Do you need to do anything to prepare for these events or tasks to make sure they go well? Is there anything not yet on your calendar that you would like to see happen? These might be steps toward your larger professional goals, or those important but not urgent things that you'd like to spend more time on. If you think of something you'd like to see happen, you can create a time on your calendar for it, or simply put it as a task on your priority list, meaning you'll get to it during some open time.

(Yes, you need open time—but that's a subject for a different section.)

Then you repeat this process with your personal life. What is on your calendar involving family and friends? How about things that you personally find enjoyable or meaningful? Do you need to do anything to prepare for these events or to make sure they go well? Is there anything not yet on your calendar that you would like to see happen? Again, you can create times on your calendar for these things, or write them as tasks on your priority list.

During this planning session, you should also look at your obligations for the week that don't rise to the level of top priorities. Do you have a plan and time allotted to tackle everything? Take a moment to think about logistics. Try to spot any potential problems. What might go wrong? Do you need to move anything or cancel anything? Can you minimize anything that is not a big priority? Do you need help with anything? What are you looking forward to?

I don't write everything that I plan to do on my priority list. Some things happen automatically—another subject we'll cover in a minute. Because automatic things don't make the list, the priority list can be short. Indeed, I think it *should* be short. Everything should fit on one notebook page. That's because the act of making a weekly priority list should itself be a decision. Barring disaster, anything that goes on the list will happen. A ringmaster needs to trust that she can keep her promises to herself. Since life happens, and gusts of wind may blow a trapeze off its usual course, that means the list needs to be limited. At the end of the week everything will be crossed off, or will be intentionally scheduled to a new time.

I know that life seldom goes exactly according to plan. Things get canceled. New things come up. I spend five minutes at the end of each workday making a more detailed plan for the next day based on this more current sense of what the day's schedule will be and based on what I've gotten done and still need to do. But the fact that things change is not an argument against planning, because having a plan means you know how to pivot when you need to. When the wi-fi goes out in the house for a week, rendering your home office unusable, you know what's most important to work on while you've decamped to Starbucks.

Knowing that you've thought through the most likely scenarios and that you will make progress on your goals even when things go awry can give you an incredible sense of calm. There may be tigers leaping through hoops in one ring, and a clown juggling in another, but this activity doesn't faze you. You know that the tigers and clowns are supposed to be there. You know what they're supposed to do, and that the trained monkeys are waiting in the wings. What needs to happen will happen, and you are calmly in charge of it all.

2. Set your rules

If you have a complex life, you need a plan. But a key part of making this sustainable is having lots of life happen *without* active planning. Complex organizations tend to cope with complexity by having what are often called "house rules" that guide expected behavior. The goal is that no one has to think much about it. Corporations have their standard operating procedures. The military has all sorts of things that are done the way they are done. Wise people with complicated lives also tend to have a lot of guidelines and systems that limit the amount of mental energy daily life requires. They notice recurring pain points, figure out repeatable solutions, and disseminate the rules so everyone can follow them. This drastically reduces the mental load of running a household—or managing a team at work—and allows other people to take on real responsibility for tasks. That way the ring-master can save their effort for where it is most needed.

The plethora of possible house rules is why I've long been fascinated by large family logistics. Back in 2002, when I was an intern at *USA Today*, I got myself assigned to write a feature piece about mega families that opened with all their laundry tips. This was before I had kids. Indeed, it was before I had ever done laundry for anyone but myself. I just loved the idea that people had systems for keeping complex things orderly, so the circus kept humming along.

Now as I manage my own large household, I lean on all sorts of house rules.

For instance, around here, Monday is pasta night. No one wants to think about dinner on Monday. Everyone loves pasta. Hence, Monday's entree is pasta, with the result that everyone is fed and no one complains.

During any given stretch of time, we tend to have a standing rotation of other meals as well. Tuesday is often chicken jazzed up in some fashion, such as with rice and a jar of sauce from the international aisle, or perhaps as fajitas served with a side of guacamole. Wednesday we outsource dinner, which strikes me as a reasonable way to celebrate the midpoint of the work week. Thursday is breakfast for dinner. Friday is make-your-own pizza night. On weekends there is more flexibility, so that is the opportunity for anything complicated, though I'm a fan of grilling a bunch of steaks that I can then incorporate into my lunches all week. Children can buy lunch at school or bring a lunch. The house rule is that the adults will pack a lunch for you if you choose up until age eight, and then you are on your own.

As for laundry, all children have a cloth laundry hamper in their rooms for dirty clothes. Clean clothes go in plastic laundry baskets, so there is no possibility that clean clothes will be put on a bed, and then transferred to the floor, where they appear dirty so they wind up back in the hamper. When possible, I suggest doing each person's laundry separately. This eliminates any need to sort, which, if you think about it, tends to be one of the major time sucks in the laundry process. If you combine two people's laundry, it is best to combine people who are completely different sizes and/or genders to make the sorting process brainless. We have bins labeled with all the sizes of children's clothes, and as children outgrow clothes, those that are still wearable go in the bins. We then "shop" from the bins before shopping for real.

Of course, socks are sometimes hard to tell apart by size, which is why I love Connie Klenke's one-time house rule. This Texas-based mother of seven children, now mostly out of the house, would label the oldest child's socks with a single dot (Sharpie style). The second oldest child got two dots. The upside of this system is that if socks were ever passed down—often the case for ski socks or soccer socks—you could simply add the appropriate number of additional dots (Connie later switched to a system where everyone got small mesh bags for socks, meaning she could stop worrying about sorting).

The Klenke family also had a house rule on vacations, which is that most summers they spent a few weeks vacationing in South Bend, Indiana. Now, having spent my teenage years living in South Bend, Indiana, I can attest that this isn't a common vacation destination. But some children would do sports camps at Notre Dame, and mom and dad and the others would do bike rides along the St. Joseph River, visit the College Football Hall of Fame, and experience less sweltering summer weather. They drove from Houston in a 15-passenger van with a giant cooler (stocked to minimize the need to stop for food or beverages), and when they did stop, it was a house rule that everyone had to visit the restroom.

Connie also made home life a little more orderly by instituting what she called Sibling Power Hours two to three times a week in the summers. During these hours, each older child would be paired up with a younger child. They'd do some sort of project together, like baking, practicing a gymnastics trick, or putting on a puppet show for everyone else. In order not to spend her life at the grocery store, Connie had a house rule that she would attempt to go only once per week, always on Mondays, buying five gallons of milk at a time. Yes, it's possible: the plastic jugs "all fit in the bottom of the cart if you turn them just the right way."

Kristen Burgess, a Traverse City, Michigan–based single mother of eight kids (with some grown), likewise relies on systems and routines to keep her circus organized. She was "in survival mode for quite a while," she tells me, following the sudden end of her marriage a few years ago. But after a rocky stretch, she figured out how to complete her bachelor's degree and restart the business she'd been running prior to the family's crisis, all while homeschooling her children. "I juggle a lot," she notes. "I make a lot of mistakes . . . but on the whole, I feel like systems and routines have really helped me and the kids thrive."

She, too, plans her weeks on Fridays, keeping an eye on all three rings. "I look at the coming week. What do I need to do for the kids, for myself, and trying to rebuild my business?" She aims to minimize active planning through several house rules. For instance, each of the older kids is responsible for cooking dinner fairly regularly. Kristen has a list of 30 of the family's favorite meals, and the child in charge chooses one of those, puts in the grocery requests, and Kristen puts in a Walmart order on Friday afternoon for pickup on Monday night. The children all have a set chore schedule of who does what on each day. The house rule is that they stick with this schedule for a year. People get used to it, but also know any annoyances aren't truly eternal. In a year they'll do something else.

Kristen works in the mornings from 5:00 to 9:00 a.m. on her business, managing a website devoted to pregnancy and birth, and some other writing. The kids know the house rule that they are not to bother her until the end of that window. Then it's time for homeschooling lessons for the rest of the morning, with afternoons a bit more free form. There is time for being outside, or chores, or other things. When we first talked, Kristen was working downtown on Tuesdays at a different job, with the older children covering (as a homeschooling family, they could simply do lessons at a different time). They were also covering Tuesday evenings, which would be Kristen's time to go on a date or see friends.

Indeed, having a routine time when a primary parent can have time for himself or herself—ensuring the existence of that third ring—is the house rule that may best keep the circus sustainable. Brittany White, cohost of the *Deliberate Motherhood* podcast, lives in the Florida panhandle with her husband and seven children. She notes that "feeding your people three times a day is somewhat of a feat." After her sixth child arrived, she decided to get serious about meal planning and, more specifically, planning one week's meals at a time in order to generate a comprehensive grocery list. She also decided always to go grocery shopping on Wednesday night. "Come anything that could happen short of a funeral I'm going shopping Wednesday evening," she says. And this is key: She goes grocery shopping solo. "I go for as long as I need to," she says. It could be hours. Indeed, sometimes she'll sit in the parking lot taking a leisurely phone call with a friend before she hits the store.

She also has a standing date to meet a friend early Sunday morning. They hang out from 6:00 a.m. to 9:00 or 10:00, sometimes painting together, sometimes talking, sometimes playing games. Both stretches of personal time have the important virtue of getting her out of the house. "It doesn't matter how many times I say 'don't interrupt me,'" she says. "The kids are still going to come ask for your attention." It is a house rule that Mom is just not available. Everyone figures it out.

Now I know that most people are not managing a household of seven-plus people. But the same mindset applies in other circumstances too. Perhaps you are managing a work team of seven-plus people—and so you can likewise set "house rules" for your squad. Perhaps all meetings end 10 minutes before the hour. Perhaps you take a direct report out to lunch every Wednesday, and (like Kurt the pastor) you have "office hours" two afternoons a week when people can reach you with no appointment, thus limiting interruptions at other times. Perhaps you create a time block for marketing every Tuesday so you don't forget to do it. Whatever it is you want to do, create a rule so you don't have to think about it, and life will start to feel more seamless.

3. Secure your net

Good systems make a complex life possible. Still, things can go wrong for any ringmaster. At a circus a few years ago I was watching acrobats do stunts on horseback when one performer tumbled. The good news: There were precautions in place to keep her from falling under the horse, and the performers (including the horses) all immediately reverted to a holding pattern, moving in a slow circle until it was clear that she was all right. Just like the Flying Cortes members train themselves to land in the net, everyone knew what was supposed to happen. That way, something going awry didn't result in catastrophe.

It's smart, and yet contrast this with the way many people treat the unexpected. People are shocked when it rains. They wonder how it could possibly happen that the basement sprang a leak, or a flight was canceled, or there was a power outage at school when a tree fell on a nearby line, and so the kids needed to be picked up at the worst possible moment. Sometimes these events turn a day's schedule chaotic, and sometimes they mean people don't make progress on their goals because "something happened." But life always happens. This should not be a surprise. These stories should not serve as the opening anecdotes for essays on how life is unknowable and it is pointless to plan for the future. True ringmasters build their schedules to allow for the possibility that life will happen. They train into the net.

We can allow grace for others and ourselves, for sure. Things will be forgotten. People will be late. But we can also create lives where the net is exactly where it is supposed to be—in other words, lives with a lot of resiliency.

This resiliency can take many forms—though in particular it helps to think through life's biggest decisions with an eye toward creating a strong net. For example, a few larger families I know have consciously purchased homes within a short walking distance of their children's schools. That way, any kid over age 10 or so can get themselves home from school whenever they need to get home. If softball practice gets out late it doesn't affect the entire family's driving schedule.

One reason many families with young kids wind up living near extended family is that—provided the family members are aiming to be helpful—someone can then come stay with the kids on short notice. Dad may be stuck in traffic and Mom's flight is delayed, but maybe Grandpa can make school pickup. Maybe he can even start boiling the water for mac and cheese so dinner happens at the usual time.

Extended family members, or the chosen family of close friends, can provide a net in all kinds of situations. Your car breaks down, so you borrow your aunt and uncle's second vehicle (which they don't need while one of them is out of town) and still get to work only a little later than expected. You drive your kids' friends home from baseball practice when you can, and then their parents happily drive your kid home the time you're sitting in the ER with another child.

For families that need paid childcare, I usually recommend a "layered" approach to create the same schedule resiliency that other people might get from nearby relatives. If option A isn't available, what is option B? Maybe your kid usually goes to daycare, but you find two backup sitters with some during-the-day availability who you can text if you need them. Or maybe you have a full-time nanny, but your employer offers a backup care benefit at a local childcare center, so you register for that and get familiar with the process for booking a slot.

Work schedules need resiliency too. Wise project managers build in space before deadlines so if one portion of a project takes longer than expected, the entire operation isn't derailed. Maybe you've used one vendor forever, but you still know who else is in the space, and you occasionally use them for small projects so you know they'll be able to scale up if need be. Your team members generally work in the office but everyone can work from home if necessary so a snowstorm doesn't cost you a week of productivity. When my local school district was facing a bus driver staffing crunch a few years ago, I was intrigued to see the plan for what to do if too many drivers called out. This plan automatically prioritized little kids (who could not be left home alone, and for whose families a delayed pickup might be a real crisis) over older kids, who, post-Covid, brought their school-issued laptops home every day and could switch to a virtual day if that were required. The school district had figured out exactly where the net should be.

Since troubles and mistakes are inevitable, we don't want to operate so close to the edge that a mistake is a disaster. In the financial world, personal finance experts recommend building up an emergency fund so that an unexpected expense doesn't force you into debt. The time equivalent is creating more margin in life, which generally means putting more open space into your schedule. If your biggest client has last-minute changes to a project on Tuesday, you'll probably deal with those. But then where does everything that was supposed to happen on Tuesday go? If Friday is lightly scheduled, the bumped tasks can go there. If every minute is spoken for, on the other hand, you'll be borrowing time from somewhere else: nights, weekends, or the next week, which will no doubt have crises of its own. A resilient schedule has time for the known and the unexpected too.

I find it helpful to adopt the same mindset that a trapeze artist would. You hope to complete all your tricks, but if you're ever adding anything new or interesting to your set, it's possible you'll miss during a performance. And as you're learning anything new, you will most definitely miss again and again. The net can't be an afterthought. You will land in it at some point, so you want to make sure the experience of landing there will be okay.

So for anything that has significant stakes, ask what could go wrong and figure out what your next actions will be. How will you get to Cleveland if your flight is canceled? Where will you stay if you don't get that certificate of occupancy before you planned to move in? What will you do if your car doesn't start on your first day at a new job?

More importantly, aim to build a life where things going wrong as they normally go wrong is just not that big a deal. I'm not saying this is easy. But a little forethought can make you feel more calmly in control of your life, even if life is complex.

4. Manage for delight

All these practices can help you manage your three-ring circus. But any good ringmaster knows that people don't pay for tickets just to watch the performers trudge through their acts. The magic of a circus is making things that are complex or challenging appear effortless. All magic is just labor, hidden well. A circus is managed for delight. Most people in the audience at the York State Fair, wilting in that hot field, had no idea of what Commander Alexander needed to do as he shinnied down the cannon barrel, or how he had set the angle and positioned the mat. They had no idea how, after being shot out headfirst, he would need to turn his body in the air, so he would land on his back. All they knew was to count down to build the excitement, and then shriek in wonder as he flew through the sky.

You can manage for delight in your life too. When I've organized my life well I often think of my schedule as something of a performance. It is not easy to ensure that everyone has an enriching and exciting summer with a mix of camps, volunteer opportunities, and friend get-togethers. There is nothing simple about making sure five children's passports are current, with at least six months' validity, before international trips. There is no plausible version of minimalism that keeps track of my choir rehearsals, my kids' cross-country practices and swim team practices and jazz band rehearsals, and whether my husband and I both get to do our long runs on any given weekend, all while I'm managing work demands. And yet when I'm planning my schedule well, everything feels quite possible. We get to do it all! There is downtime and space for fun. A full workweek ends with going to an Olivia Rodrigo concert with my daughter Friday night, and then to the York State Fair on a Sunday, where I become so fascinated by a man getting shot out of a cannon that I decide I have to write about him.

We all delight in different things, but one way to manage your circus for delight is to make sure you always have something you are genuinely looking forward to. Yes, your well-planned schedule has everyone getting their flu shots on time and has you prepared for that sales meeting in Phoenix on Thursday. But what makes you feel in love with your life? Is there anything in your schedule that makes you giddy with excitement?

If not, go back and work on it again. Maybe you'll wind up at Phoenix's Desert Botanical Garden, wandering amid the saguaros at night after your presentation. Maybe you'll take 30 minutes to go to an art museum on a lunch break someday, or you'll schedule a Zoom chat with your college roommate after your kids go to bed.

On a practical level, one helpful tactic for making sure you have something to look forward to is to think of each weekend like a vacation. One study found that when people were instructed to treat their upcoming weekends like vacations, they wound up happier, less stressed, and more satisfied. They spent less time working and on housework. They did a few more fun things than they might have, but most important, they paid more attention to the happy things they did—perhaps feeling more like this time was special.

We all have a million things to do, but I like this finding because it suggests an easy way to discover more delight in life. Just be sure to take in the show—on weekends for sure, but also on weekday evenings (the subject of a later chapter) and any time, really. Maybe some folks want to settle for a more restrained existence, but a structurally complex life doesn't need to be chaotic. The ringmaster takes great pleasure in the performance. You can savor all that is happening as the clowns march in, the tightrope walker teeters, and a trapeze artist catches another performer's arms—just as planned, and right on time.

CHAPTER 3

DREAM BIG, PLAN SMALL

If you happened to be visiting Yellowstone National Park in mid-August 2023, perhaps staying at Canyon Lodge & Cabins, or taking in the Lamar Valley and Old Faithful, you might have spotted the DeCou family gawking at these wonders with you. Kristin and Rob, and their two elementary school age children, spent a few days in the park then. They had visited the Grand Tetons right before.

It's a fairly common summer vacation, but what distinguishes the DeCou family's Yellowstone trip is that it came in the middle of a multiyear quest to see all 63 of America's national parks—from Acadia to Zion.

The family had always liked their outdoor adventures. Rob has completed several long trail races, for instance, but in 2022, Kristin recalls, her husband had "invited me to think bigger." They'd discovered the American Field Trip family, travel influencers who'd visited all the national parks in 18 months. They wondered whether this feat might be possible for their own family.

So they began scheming. A little reflection helped them see that they weren't in a position to quit their jobs and homeschool on the road, which is what covering that much distance over that short of a time frame might require. But Rob, who was then working as a business instructor at a community college as well as on some entrepreneurial ventures, could reasonably take the summers off. Kristin could scale down her home-organizing business for a few months over the summer as well. It was often a slow time anyway, so she could push more projects to the school year. Since they lived near Olympic National Park in Washington State, they could rent their house out each summer if they weren't there. Back-of-the-envelope calculations revealed that the rent could fund most of their travel. They wouldn't see all the parks in 18 months, but by repurposing slower weeks, they could do so over the next several years.

That left the logistics. A lot of logistics. Kristin and crew constructed a giant spreadsheet based on when they could score accommodations near in-demand places or stay with friends and family; how far they'd need to travel between stops; and what all this would cost. "The first summer we didn't go to that many popular parks," Kristin says. That's because they tend to book up far in advance. But there are often hotels near the parks, and KOA (Kampgrounds of America) campgrounds, which are blessed places with wi-fi for the adults, playgrounds for kids, and washing machines for everyone. "Most people assume you need an RV, but we ended up doing some research and purchased an SUV and used a roof tent," Kristin says. That way they could drive fairly normally between places and camp when they needed to. They'd pack a week's worth of outfits and do laundry every four to five days.

And so, in 2022, off they went. That first June they started at Crater Lake National Park in Oregon, then headed south to Mount Lassen National Park in Manzanita, California. They made a stop at their Grandma Holly's house in California before hitting Redwood National Park. Then it was off to Great Basin

National Park before taking a 6 hour and 33 minute drive (410 miles) to the Grand Canyon, where they stayed at the Grand Canyon Railway Hotel. A few days and 182 miles later, they were staying at an Airbnb property and seeing Petrified Forest National Park. Then it was on to Four Corners, and Mesa Verde, and eventually through the Dakotas, and on to Voyageurs National Park in Minnesota, and the Indiana Dunes, before they made it back to the West Coast and the start of the school year. In case you were wondering: No, the children were not naturally angelic on these long drives. But the DeCous came up with the rule that tablets could be used only while the family was driving. "That was a game changer. They would look forward to hitting the road," Kristin reports.

With the experience of knowing how to book ahead in national parks, the next summer they looped through other places, getting to camp in Yosemite National Park and Kings Canyon, and staying at the Ranch at Death Valley. They went to the Utah parks, and through the ever popular and ever crowded Grand Tetons, Yellowstone, and Glacier before heading back to Washington and school and work. By the next summer, they had hit 50 of the 63 parks by using shorter school breaks too, so they headed out to Hawaii to visit those parks. When I circled back with Kristin in early 2025, the family was about to embark on a spring-break cruise, where an excursion would take them to the US Virgin Islands National Park. Their summer travel itinerary involved visiting the Alaska parks you can drive to. The ones you need to fly into would be next, and then National Park of American Samoa, though that was going to require time to save up for. But they had a path to being done by 2026 or 2027 (which they were documenting on their website, WildParksFamily.com and on Instagram as @wildparksfamily).

There were tough moments for sure. "It is hard traveling with kids, and living out of our car, and sleeping on the rooftop,"

Kristin notes. She recalled one night when they arrived at their campground late and popped up the tent in the rain, and heard the zippers of other people's sleeping bags in a maddening percussive symphony all night long. I should mention that all four DeCous were sleeping on a single king-size mattress. "I was wishing I was staying in a lodge. I was wishing we had different options," she notes. Everything had been booked, so there they were, just trying to make the most of it.

But there were also sublime moments in unexpected places. That first summer they spent a day in Theodore Roosevelt National Park, a lesser-known stop in North Dakota. As the sun was setting, they watched, awestruck, as more than 300 bison lumbered across the rustic landscape. They spotted wild turkeys and foxes, and felt almost as if they had traveled back in time. "We were the only ones there," she says. "When you're watching a geyser in Yellowstone with 500 people, it's not as majestic." But this was amazing. "That was the park that surprised us all."

If they hadn't been trying to see everything, they never would have gone there. "Having the defined purpose of seeing all the parks, it brings you places you wouldn't have gone otherwise," she says. "You don't know what you don't know."

❋

WE ALL HAVE THE SAME AMOUNT OF TIME. WE ALL HAVE 24 HOURS in a day, 168 hours in a week, and 8,760 hours in a year. If we track where the time goes, we soon see that everyone has some discretionary time, even if it comes in bits and pieces.

Unfortunately, the usual experience is of muddling along, spending these bits of time without much direction. We tell ourselves we have no time because much of the time we do have is not memorable. There is little connection between one day's discretionary time and another's. Or else we seem stuck in a time loop: reading the same website's headlines, checking comments on something else. Even longer stretches of discretionary time are seldom considered holistically. This year's paid time off has nothing to do with time off four summers from now.

In this chapter, though, I hope to convince you that by connecting these dots of discretionary time—even just a little bit—you can make big things possible.

People overestimate what they can do in the short run. They underestimate what they can do in the long run. Many daunting projects can be completed over a finite amount of time simply by breaking the journey into smaller steps. You dream big and plan small. You never tackle too much at once. Nothing feels onerous. But as the days keep passing, even little things add up. This is true with a project like visiting all the national parks over a few years, or perhaps over a decade if you have a less flexible schedule, but is also true for reading big things (say, all the works of Shakespeare), writing big things (hundreds of sonnets, perhaps), listening to something extensive (all the works of Bach?), learning something new, or whatever you choose to take on.

There are ways to make a given project more feasible, like knowing to get a pop-up tent for your SUV, or where the KOA campgrounds are. But none of that is particularly difficult if you learn a few strategies for planning a big journey, which is what this chapter covers.

I promise that this is all simple, which is good, because there is great joy in the discipline of collecting time's ephemera over a big and expansive number of days. Not only can you do big things worth doing, even in the middle of a busy life, you can be the happy beneficiary of a time paradox. Putting big and worthwhile things into a schedule actually makes you feel like you have more time, because in your mind, you become the kind of person who has the time to do big and worthwhile things.

You have time to visit all the national parks, or learn to read the New Testament in Greek, or write a memoir. Time feels abundant when much feels possible, no matter how much else you have going on.

Anywhere is walking distance

My interest in long projects began, fittingly enough, with *War and Peace*. Leo Tolstoy's epic of the Napoleonic Wars in Russia should be known for its richly developed characters and sweeping scope, but I would say that for most people it is simply known for being a big book. My Signet Classics edition has 1,455 pages. English translations clock in at around 570,000 words. With such heft, simply having time to read Tolstoy becomes a statement of how much space one must have in life. Martha Beck graciously provided a blurb for one of my earlier time-management books in which she joked that the manuscript "convinced me I had time to read it. Then it convinced me I had time to reread *War and Peace*."

I'd plowed through the book years ago, admittedly skimming a lot, but I'd remembered it being surprisingly entertaining. Then, in late 2020, Jeremy Anderberg of the Read More Books newsletter shared this fact: *War and Peace* is comprised of 361 short chapters. You might recall that there are 365 days in a year. He planned to read a chapter of *War and Peace* each day through 2021. I pulled my copy off the shelf to check and, sure enough, each chapter was only about four pages long. Even in the small font of the Signet Classic, I could read four pages in 10 minutes or less. From tracking my time, I was well aware that I spent more than 10 minutes each day reading comments on snarky social media posts or simply staring off into space. If I stuck with the project, and used a bit of time ephemera each day for the same thing, rather than random things, I would finish the book on December 27.

And so I was in. I read a chapter on January 1. I read another on January 2, and January 3. If I was in my office I read the Signet Classic as I sat down to work each morning, but if I was traveling I read on the Kindle app, having downloaded *War and Peace*'s digital bulk for the bargain price of 99 cents.

It was wonderful. At that pace I could read carefully. I felt no need to race through, thus missing little details Tolstoy sprinkled in like wildflowers growing by one of those rutted roads in the Russian countryside. I did not get bogged down in the Freemasonry bit, or even the Battle of Borodino, as readers are wont to do, because if a day was a slog, it was only a short slog. Just a few pages. If I missed a day, I didn't have much to catch up on, because it was only a few pages. I delighted in the occasional timely matchups, like Tolstoy writing of the melting snow and coming spring as I read on a May day, or the deepening cold after the French took Moscow and the weather marched toward winter in my world too. The promise was that if I read a chapter a day I would finish. Time kept passing, and my bookmark kept moving forward, and on December 27, I did.

I mean, of course, right? Reading 361 chapters in 361 days gets us there, and yet there was something magical about the process. It felt so light and easy. Reading the last pages made me giddy (even if one is indulging Tolstoy his philosophy, not a story, by the end). I'd kept my promise and time kept its promise: Over big enough stretches of time, you can do anything.

Not really, of course. But there is a saying that anywhere is walking distance if you have the time, and with that mindset, over the last few years I've completed many yearlong projects— I've read all the works of Shakespeare and all the works of Jane Austen, I've listened to all the (known) works of Bach, written hundreds of sonnets in iambic pentameter, and other such things.

I've seen other people finally make the time to write a novel, or train for a pilgrimage, or read sacred texts. You, too, can use the same approach to tackle a big project and achieve a sense of time abundance. After all, if you have time to read *War and Peace*, you can't truly be starved for time, right? You are experiencing big time—big enough for the biggest books and anything else.

How to do something big

When I first started evangelizing about my yearlong projects, and how others might make time for similar things, someone summed up this message as "Oh, you're helping people learn to stick with habits." On some level, reading a chapter of *War and Peace* each day is a habit, but there is some nuance here, because not all habits are created equal. Even if you don't think of yourself as the kind of person who sticks with habits, when we dream big and plan small enough, we move out of the realm of who is disciplined and who isn't, and out of the necessity for intricate accountability strategies, and into the truth that many small things are quite easy to do. People who find it challenging to stick with a goal to run four times a week often do brush their teeth every single day. No one points to their daily tooth brushing as evidence of their ironclad discipline. Nor, in the other direction, do people try to weasel out of brushing their teeth with the excuse that they're on vacation, or it's their birthday. Tooth brushing is easy, relatively pleasant, doesn't take much time, has a compelling value proposition, and tends to happen around the same time each day with any aberrations planned for (e.g., people pack their toothbrush when they travel).

I maintain that if you can brush your teeth 361 days in a row, which you probably have, you can read 361 very short passages in a row—if you want to do it. More complex projects, like visiting all the national parks, are likewise doable if the steps are straightforward and fit into your life as it is or reasonably could be. You simply need to make sure you choose your projects well, you need to make sure the steps are well defined, and you need to figure out how to troubleshoot if your motivation flags. But you don't have to quit your job. You don't have to disrupt your life. You don't have to wake up at 5:00 a.m. You just teach an extra class during the year to make up for the summer income. You take the kids on a road trip rather than putting them in a local day camp. If the project is compelling enough, there are a few things you can do to make it feel as feasible as brushing your teeth.

1. Choose well

The first step to undertaking a long journey is making sure the destination is somewhere you want to go. Sometimes you know this. It's something you've wanted to do for ages, like reading all of Shakespeare if you've got a thing for Elizabethan literature.

But often, I think people don't stick with long-term projects because they don't actually want to do them. They sound good in theory, but they don't feel appealing in the doing. If you don't like spending time in the great outdoors, rain and mosquitos included, seeing all the national parks won't be the project for you. I am not a movie person, so I won't spend a year watching through a list of the 100 greatest movies of all time. There are infinite ways people can spend their time, and sticking with anything big and self-chosen long enough to see it through is going to require wanting to do it not just when you are your best self, but when you are dealing with all manner of crises that life will throw at you.

So consider carefully. If you think completing a big project like listening to all of Beethoven, reading all the works of Robert Caro, or visiting all the major league baseball parks sounds intriguing, then come up with potential ideas, and spend some time thinking through them before you commit. Do your research. Has anyone else done this? What was it like? Try a bit yourself if you haven't (we'll talk more about test-driving later). If you are thinking you might listen to all of Wagner's music, listen to two hours of an opera while you're on a long car trip, or attend a performance if you can find one. I now spend time in November and December each year thinking through what sounds exciting enough to incorporate into my daily life.

One gut-check question to ask about any long-term project is this: Would I do this on vacation?

If your long-term project involves travel (like the DeCou family's excursions, or perhaps visiting all the state capitals at a rate of five per year over the next decade), then obviously these vacations have to sound fun. But it's the same for any other big project. People who are excited to train for long races do generally figure out how they can run on vacations. They run on hotel treadmills or do loops around the cruise ship deck. They get up before their families and run before the day's sightseeing. Maybe not every day, but they tend not to take a week off and, more importantly, they aren't looking toward that vacation time as a guilt-free opportunity to get a week off.

For something to be doable long term, you will need to be willing to call upon your problem-solving abilities to find ways to do it on days that aren't normal for some reason. You can't be using your problem-solving abilities to look for reasons not to do it. People who stick with projects they take on tend to put their potential goals through this rubric before they decide to commit.

I'm not saying every day will be great (think: Freemasonry section of *War and Peace*), but you want the day-to-day journey to be enjoyable enough that you're not looking to get out of it.

Zoe Barinaga, an executive in the oil and gas industry, set a goal recently to walk the Camino de Santiago pilgrimage in Spain. This project required months of training to be able to walk many miles on varying terrain. Spain is obviously a compelling destination, but Zoe made the training a lot more enjoyable by doing it with her husband. They'd schedule two long walks each weekend (with a couple of smaller walks completed individually during the week), exploring various routes in their community. "The journey to getting ready for the pilgrimage was motivating," she says. "The pilgrimage was the end goal, but we looked forward to our weekly walks because we were doing it together." They also listened to a "Bible in a year" app together while training (each of them wearing one ear bud!) to keep their focus on the spiritual aspect of the pilgrimage.

Projects tend to be more compelling if they have a true destination—that is, a finish line (something that distinguishes long-term projects from the way we normally think about habits). This is one reason I'm drawn toward choosing yearlong projects each year. December 31 is an obvious end point. "All the works of Shakespeare" or "all the works of Bach" are also finish lines, even if there are scholarly questions of what is canonical or spurious. So, for instance, I decided that I would listen to the 1,080 pieces in the main part of the Bach-Werke-Verzeichnis (BWV) catalogue in 2024. When I read Shakespeare in 2022, I read through a 1,023-page anthology that at least billed itself as being the complete works.

Less definitive finish lines can work, but it still helps to have a sense of what constitutes success. Starting in December 2022, Ottawa resident Elizabeth Howell, a Canadian who's a freelance journalist and whose current job involves communications, decided to learn Latin well enough to be able to read Julius Caesar in his original language. When she achieved that, she kept studying Latin, but added a new goal of learning enough ancient Greek to be able to read biblical Greek (much of the New Testament was written in that language). You could spend a lifetime studying either of those languages, but being able to understand the gist of a chapter—particularly one written for the masses, as Caesar and Paul were doing—is reasonably straightforward.

Of course, even if you define a project well, and it feels compelling, it may not go as you wish. This is the nature of experimentation. In 2022, I set a goal to write 100- to 200-word scenes daily that followed a character through a single day in her life. It could have worked. At the end of the year I would theoretically have had a 50,000-word novella, written in compelling little chunks, about this modern-day Ulysses. But my pacing was off. It was 2:00 p.m. on Bloomsday by mid-March, which meant I was really stretching out the remaining hours of the day, and the plot never took off in a coherent fashion. I stuck with the project, because I am a stubborn person, but when I went back through what I'd written, I was bored and annoyed.

Oh well. The good news is I can now confirm I had more than one year left to live, and all of this is just for fun anyway. When something doesn't work as you intend, you can try something else. While it's important to choose well, project-choosing turns out to be a skill like anything else, and we get better at choosing over time as we learn more about ourselves. So in 2023 I switched gears and set a goal to write 52 sonnets over the course of the year at a rate of one per week (two lines a day in iambic pentameter, following a certain rhyming scheme). With a clean slate each Sunday, I only had to stick with a bad sonnet until Saturday. Then I could take a shot at writing something else. It was just a much better way to experiment. Indeed, I enjoyed that project so much that I reupped for 2024 and 2025.

2. Define your steps and create your calendar

Shira Gill, a professional home organizer, and author of *Minimalista*, has organized countless homes at this point. "The biggest challenge people face is just feeling paralyzed because of the too-muchness of it," she says. Faced with a mess and over-flowing closets, people think they need to take several weeks off work to organize their homes.

Of course, few people get that kind of time off for that kind of task, and if they do take that kind of sabbatical, they tend to want to do things that don't involve their junk drawers. So by the time they call Shira, they are feeling overwhelmed. No one, she notes, ever calls her and says they've been methodically working through their home at a rate of 20 minutes a day. That's because anyone doing that might not need to call her, as that is basically what she coaches people to do: "Break the big thing into lots of little things," she says. "One room at a time. Within the room you will literally do one drawer or one shelf or counter at a time." In a normal-size home, perhaps you might identify 100 spots that need your attention. At a gentle rate of five a week, allowing for days off and the inevitability of life's crises, you could organize an entire home in five months of time ephemera, or less, as long as you stuck with it. Those five months are going to pass one way or another. At the end, you could have an organized home. Or not. The difference between an organized home and a not-organized home is really not that much each day, but this is also true: cumulatively, the difference between nothing and just a little more than nothing turns out to be huge.

So it goes with anything else. You may not want to organize your home. But once you have dreamed up a big project that seems exciting, if it is not already broken down for you (e.g., 361 chapters in 361 days), you need to break this down into an appropriate number of steps that will make it doable for your life. How much time can you sustainably devote to your project?

Perhaps you will aim for daily, which is easy to remember, or you might aim for 3 or 4 times a week (this might be more feasible if some days are much busier for you than others).

If you're aiming for daily, don't think about how much time you could find on a perfect day. Think about a day when you have to leave work early to pick up a sick kid and then you lose power in the afternoon and it doesn't come on again until close to midnight. How much time could you devote to your project on a day like *that*? What about on a day when you're traveling for work and have meetings stacked back-to-back and a dinner with a talkative client afterward? Or when you're visiting extended family and have people around you constantly? None of these are true aberrations. There are no typical weeks. If you've got a busy life, and don't have complete control over your time, most sustainable habits can't take more than 30 minutes a day, and in many cases, less than that is more reasonable. But that is fine. Twenty minutes a day, if it's truly daily, is about 120 hours in a year—the equivalent of taking three weeks off work to devote to your goal, without actually having to do that.

If you tracked your time after reading chapter 1, look back to see where there is generally discretionary space, or space that could be repurposed, or even multitasked. You might listen to Bach in the car, as I did during 2024, or the audiobook of *War and Peace*. Sometimes a project requires different kinds of work, which means that you can use different chunks of time if you are intentional about it. Elizabeth Howell hired tutors to help her work through that classic Latin textbook, Ørberg's *Familia Romana*, but she also listens to Latin podcasts during her downtime. "Ten minutes at a time, five minutes at a time, it all adds up," she says. "Most of us can find thirty minutes a day in five-minute or ten-minute increments."

Once you've figured out how much space you're aiming for, you can decide how many steps you'll need to take to finish your journey, and their size. The smaller the step, the easier this will be to fit into life, though the longer the overall project will be. This is a personal choice, dependent on circumstance. If you want to see games in all 30 of the major league baseball parks, but you only get two weeks off your in-office job each year plus major holidays, this is just going to take longer than if you had a more flexible schedule. That said, it's probably still doable, and in either scenario you'll need to plan out how you'll get to all these places. Just as any long journey requires a map that will reliably deliver you where you are going, any big project requires a calendar you can follow that clearly delineates each step. That way, you'll know for sure that you've done what you're supposed to do each day, or perhaps over each long weekend if you're traveling, and you'll know what's coming up on future days.

If you're lucky, there might already be a calendar out there in the world. For instance, there are several "Shakespeare in a year" calendars online, and I followed the listening instructions of a website called the Complete Beethoven in 2025. A good calendar can keep you from foundering. Many an eager Christian has set out to read the Bible in a year, only to get lost in Leviticus or, if they make it through that trial, to get stuck in the swamps of Numbers or Deuteronomy. At a steady pace, you don't reach Jesus and the New Testament until fall. That's why wise shepherds have created Bible-reading calendars that combine a reading from the Old Testament with one from the New Testament to keep people interested.

I used existing calendars for my first longer projects, but by a few years in, I decided I could create my own. Reading all of Jane Austen was straightforward. I purchased a seven-volume set of her complete novels and juvenilia, which had about 3,000 pages including notes, and a paperback compilation of her unfinished works. I went in chronological order of publication and read about 10 pages per day. Bach was more complicated. Listening to 1,080 works in a year would theoretically mean listening to three per day. But some of those 1,080 pieces are one-minute chorales, while a performance of all six parts of the Christmas Oratorio (BWV 248) could clock in at close to three hours. Eventually I decided to create a spreadsheet that assigned each day a piece or two from the first half of the BWV catalog (1 to 524, which is the vocal music), and the second half (525 to 1080, which is the instrumental music). My goal was 30 to 40 minutes of music each day, and so if a work was 90 minutes I would stretch it over three days. I hit the end in late November, which left space for revisiting favorites, wading into the post-1,080 pieces (it's a long story), and figuring out the next year's project.

Creating a calendar takes time. Kristin DeCou spent many hours creating each summer's national parks itinerary, with notes on how far an Airbnb was from the next KOA campground, but doing so *massively* increases the chances of success. If a few days are tedious, a calendar keeps your eye on the goal. Jane Austen's *Mansfield Park* is not known for being the world's most exciting read. But at a pace of 10 pages a day, I knew I would finish this 439-page book exactly 44 days after I started. I could see that date on the calendar.

To make sure your calendar is workable, you should test-drive it for a few days before you officially start your project. With yearlong goals, I often think of November and December as "resolutions preseason." You practice without it really counting. This prep work helps you figure out what a big project would look like in your life, and may help you troubleshoot. You can choose a few random future days' assignments and do them, just as if you were doing them for real. Hopefully you'll see that the project works in life as it really is—and that can give you confidence that you'll be able to stick with the thing.

3. Persist and reward yourself

A calendar is easier to stick with than a vague goal. In 2024, I wasn't just listening to Bach here and there. I knew that "On February 12 I will listen to BWV 43, which is a 21-minute cantata, BWV 589, which is a 5-minute organ piece, and BWV 590, which is a 12-minute organ piece." I put those assignments on my to-do list for the day alongside everything else. Today I will record a podcast, write two newsletters, sign up for parent-teacher conferences, and listen to BWV 43, 589, and 590. If your days are tightly scheduled, then identify the exact time when you will take your small steps. Early is good. Identify a backup slot in case the first spot is taken away from you. Keep the steps small enough that if you miss a day for some reason, taking two steps on another day won't feel overwhelming. It's better not to miss five days in a row, but if you do, doubling up for the next five days gets you current without too much fuss.

If you've chosen well and done your test-driving, persistence should feel doable. For projects involving travel, you're going to go somewhere anyway, so this should feel like small changes on the margin. As for daily long-term projects, you brushed your teeth today, right? You likely showered as well. If you're a coffee drinker, you procured a cup of coffee in some fashion and drank it. These things don't take zero time, but you did them, and you will do them tomorrow too, and you don't think much about them. You don't belabor *if* you're going to do them, it's just a matter of *when*. This is how we stick with things long term. They are simply part of the day. They feel easy enough. Indeed, with a long project, if you choose small enough steps, some days will feel almost too easy. *War and Peace* has chapters that are just two pages long. Is this cheating? Two lines in a sonnet is a mere 20 syllables. When the project itself is massive, sometimes the temptation is not to accept this ease and to feel like you should do more.

Please, resist this temptation. When you race ahead, unless you can actually see the finish line, the pace stops being sustainable. Plus, if you get ahead, you might be tempted to start skipping days, and then you can lose momentum. Better to keep going with just a little more than nothing, knowing that the difference between nothing and a little more than nothing is cumulatively great. Some literature on habits suggests that starting small is good because you can scale up over time, but when we are working with big time, then it's fine to stay small. The promise you make to yourself is that you won't attempt more on the easy days so you are able to ask yourself for the same step on the harder days. Time then keeps its promise that you will finish exactly when the calendar says you will. There's no need to rush this along.

There's also no need to get discouraged on the ho-hum days. It is human nature to have more enthusiasm at the start of any project, and at the end, when the finish line *is* in sight. People make motivational posters with the saying "A journey of 1,000 miles begins with a single step," but I don't think we need motivational posters about the first step. You're raring to go for the first step. It's around the 568,675th step when people forget why they started, or get fixated on how far they still have to go. So don't think about that. Time passes one way or another. Just walk the mile you're in, just like you'd walk any other mile, and also know that it is often in the mushy middle when moments of magic happen. Watch for these. Pay attention. With my two-lines-of-iambic-pentameter-each-day project I'd write four terrible sonnets over the course of the month. Then I'd get an idea and write something I liked more, like this poem, called "Sweet Nothings."

> Before the stars, before the planets set
> into their orbits, which define a day
> and year, then what was time? The alphabet
> came after words, one might still chance to say
>
> "I love you" never knowing what was "v"
> or "l," or what it meant to write a thought.
> These constructs come after the thing, we see
> our rules imposed on things existing not
>
> because of rules. And yet, how good to know
> that if we say we'll meet at 3 p.m.,
> at the appointed point of spin we'll go
> to our shared spot on earth and on a whim
>
> we'll write each other notes, sweet nothings, such—
> these lines that mean so little and so much.

You can keep the faith, knowing that it is in the pursuit of completion that the sublime can catch you by surprise. Kristin DeCou's family would never have visited Theodore Roosevelt National Park if they weren't trying to see all the parks. It's not Yellowstone. It's not Yosemite. I hadn't even heard of it until she mentioned it, and yet there in nowhere North Dakota is where the stunning beauty of North America's native land-scape hit her.

To be sure, there are ways to nudge yourself along in this per-sistence, at least until the intrinsic motivation kicks back in. One of Elizabeth Howell's most surprising discoveries as she learned ancient languages was about the power of community. Latin isn't a dead language on the internet, and Elizabeth is part of "a great spoken Latin community now that includes people who play Skyrim in Latin and produce shows on cooking in Latin." There are Discord and Reddit groups that are beginner friendly, and all this means more support: "When you're laughing with somebody over a verb it feels a little less like a slog."

If you're the sort who likes to know that someone else is on a journey with you, then recruit others to join in. I've done several projects on my own, but I enjoy sharing my sonnets on my blog. Several people borrowed my Bach calendar and listened to his works just as I did.

You can also persist toward the finish line by rewarding yourself. Some rewards are obvious. As Zoe Barinaga walked through Spain, her husband told her, surprised, that she didn't look happy. She said it was because "the journey is ending and I want it to go on for longer." Coming into the Cathedral of Santiago de Compostela at the end, she reports, "It was very emotional to reach the cathedral after such a long journey. Like many, I broke down in tears." Perhaps you could watch a movie version of each of Jane Austen's novels after you finish reading each book. You could go to a performance of one of Shakespeare's plays. You could print up copies of your memoir to share with family and friends. You could gamify your steps toward your goal, perhaps giving yourself an extra $10 in your treat budget for every 10 chapters of *War and Peace* completed.

For Bach, as my reward, I chose to get to know one piece even better. I have loved Bach's Mass in B Minor since I learned it with my college choir. But I left to go study abroad in Australia before the actual concert. "Sing in the B Minor Mass" went on my bucket list. Then nearly 25 years passed as I realized that while you can buy yourself a plane ticket to Australia if that's on your bucket list, it's a lot harder to find a choir, an orchestra, and a conductor who wants to perform any given work.

But in late 2024, one of my church's staff singers, who worked as the business manager for another choir in Philadelphia, mentioned that they would be performing the Mass in B Minor on New Year's Eve. One thing led to another and I began driving downtown on Monday nights, going to St. Mark's for rehearsals, and singing the second soprano line.

Listening to Bach is amazing. Singing Bach helps you appreciate the intricacies on a whole new level: the melismas, the chromatic harmonies, the symbolism in his note placement. For instance, in the Mass in B Minor, the Sanctus splits into six-part harmony, because, our director informed us, the "holy, holy, holy" verses in the Bible that inspire this part of the mass (Isaiah 6:3 and Revelation 4:8) both come in scenes where it's mentioned that the seraphim surrounding the throne of God have six wings. Seriously. You don't know what you don't know. It's humbling seeing the work that goes into a few seconds of music.

Adding another four hours of weekly commitments into my life was a big ask. But it felt surprisingly doable, for reasons suggested by a fascinating study from Cassie Mogilner Holmes, Zoë Chance, and Michael I. Norton.

In an experiment, some subjects were assigned to edit the essays of at-risk high school students. Others were allowed to leave the lab early; that is, they got a windfall of free time. But curiously, in follow-up surveys, the folks who spent time editing the essays were less likely to view time as scarce, and more likely to say they had time to spare. It seems that feeling like you have accomplished something meaningful can make time feel more abundant.

So it goes for big journeys. When you see you have the time to learn Latin, or walk the Camino de Santiago pilgrimage, or listen to all the works of Bach, you realize that you simply can't be the kind of person who's starved for time. You have tons of time, as evidenced by the fact that you have learned Latin, walked El

Camino, or listened to all the works of Bach. If you have time to read *War and Peace*, you have time for anything else you want to do. It's just our little secret that reading *War and Peace* takes 10 minutes a day over the long haul, and many other big things don't take much time either. Your rational brain doesn't need to know that. Instead, you can experience big time and love what it makes possible.

CHAPTER 4

STOP WISHING
TIME AWAY

How do you feel about your job? How do people, in general, feel about their work?

While "how's work?" is standard small talk, it turns out to be a tricky question. Gallup often asks people about their work satisfaction levels. In 2023, 54 percent of employed respondents said they were "very satisfied" with their job or the work they did; 33 percent said they were somewhat satisfied. Back in 2013, an eyebrow-raising Gallup poll found that 68 percent of people said they would continue to work even if they won $10 million in the lottery, and the majority of these people said they would continue in the same job. This implies a high level of workplace bliss.

But as you might suspect, there is also evidence that this bliss is an illusion. One famous study asked people to report their moods as they went about their days. Activities received a score based on whether people generally used positive phrases (such as "happy" or "enjoying myself") or negative ones ("annoyed," "hassled," and so forth). With this method, the researchers found that "work" landed second from the bottom on a scale of everyday activities. Housework scored better. The evening commute scored better. The only activity that scored worse than work was the morning commute, a task whose primary flaw is that it ends with you being at your job.

These seem to be contradictory findings. Yet as we consider how people think about their time and their lives, there is a way to at least partially reconcile them.

When people reflect on how they feel about their work, their first impulse is to think about their satisfaction overall. In a free market, you can always go do something else. If you haven't, work can't be too miserable, at least on an abstract level.

On the other hand, you can know that you have a reasonably interesting job, good benefits, and friendly coworkers, and still find that 10:00 a.m. staff meeting insufferable. You keep glancing at the clock, feeling "annoyed" and "hassled" and hoping the minutes have flown faster than they actually have.

It is this hour-by-hour happiness that I am most interested in. It is this hour-by-hour satisfaction, or lack thereof, that is most ripe for improvement in our quest for relishing more of our lives.

The good news, if you are not enamored with your job, is that we spend a lower proportion of life working than we think we do. With 168 hours in a week, a 40-hour-a-week job is nowhere near the "full" amount of people's time that "full time" implies. The admonition that "you spend the majority of your waking hours at work" is just not true for most people. The average workweek in March 2025, according to the US Bureau of Labor Statistics, was about 34 hours. For someone who sleeps 8 hours a night, a 40-hour-per-week job leaves 72 waking, non-working hours each week for other things. A 50-hour-per-week job leaves 62 waking, nonworking hours for other things. This can be a life-changing realization if you're not currently thrilled with whatever it is you do.

That said, part of falling in love with a schedule means not wishing the hours of nine to five away, even if there is still plenty of time for other pursuits. I do not believe clock watching is inevitable. We may not all be astronauts, ballerinas, race-car drivers, or whatever you wanted to be when you grew up, but even in an average job it might be possible to look up and say "Oh, is it five o'clock already?"

That's because a few practical tweaks can change your experience of a normal workday. They can make you think, on a Tuesday morning commute, that you have something to look forward to, rather than simply wishing to be on the other side of the next eight hours. I have seen hundreds of people learn to feel better about their workdays. This includes people with mixed feelings about their work and people who are pretty happy. We can always be happier. Whatever you do for a living, I think you can learn to be happier too.

✳

IF FIGURING OUT WHETHER PEOPLE ARE HAPPY AT WORK IS COM-plicated, giving workplace advice is doubly so. People work in very different ways. Much work-focused productivity and time-management advice assumes a corporate environment, where people spend time managing email and attending meetings, or a creative or entrepreneurial one, where people have much control over their time. If I finish my main priority for the day, I can in fact be done. But as a nurse once put it, she could not take extra good care of her patients during the first six hours of her shift and then knock off for the second half. Or consider someone like Commander Alexander from chapter 2, whose job involves getting shot out of a cannon. There's not a lot of advice that might be applicable to him, a philosophy professor, the in-house counsel for a tech company, a flight attendant, the manager of a fast casual restaurant, or a construction site supervisor.

That said, humans are humans. We all do largely want things like feeling a sense of competence (or at least finding meaning in what we do), a sense of belonging ("relatedness" in self-determination theory), and autonomy. These desires are close to universal. It makes sense that satisfying them might lead to feeling motivated in one's work.

I can see, looking at my own life, how these factors can make some workdays and weeks more pleasant than others. I love an open work day when I can sit down with a rough draft of something longer and make it better, or, in a total surprise to my introverted self, when I can get up onstage and make people laugh (competence and meaning). I like seeing recording sessions for my *Best of Both Worlds* podcast on my calendar, because I am basically getting paid to chat with a friend (belonging). When I use my job flexibility to take interesting breaks (autonomy)—like visiting a local botanical garden to see the fall flowers and leaves—I come back to my desk much happier, and often with better ideas.

My work is different from most people's. But if we know these desires are common, then the question of how to enjoy an average Tuesday becomes a question of how to satisfy these desires in an average workweek, and in ways that feel feasible for most people. What practical actions can just about anyone do this week to start wishing fewer work hours away?

Through my conversations with people about their work, and in studying thousands of schedules, I've landed on three strategies that meet these criteria.

1. Meaning—Spend one more hour per week on the work you like most.
2. Belonging—Spend 15 more minutes per week deepening a work friendship.

3. Autonomy—Take two short, intentional breaks per day to do something that you can genuinely look forward to.

I've often suggested this "Blueprint for a Better Workday" to people with mixed feelings about their jobs, suspecting it would help, but in the course of writing this book, I decided to test these ideas more systematically. I recruited people for what I called a Better Workday Challenge—a three-week program in which people tried out these strategies and reported on their experiences. What worked? What didn't? What challenges did people face? I analyzed the responses of nearly 200 people who worked for pay 21-plus hours per week and who completed at least a certain number of the surveys I sent in the course of this challenge.

The good news is that even when people didn't implement these strategies perfectly, they were likely to wind up happier at work. They felt better about their time overall. All time is valuable, and even if you work mostly because you have to, there's no reason not to make these hours as pleasant as possible.

The Better Workday Challenge

My Better Workday Challenge ran during September and October 2024 (with some follow-up in November). As with the Time Tracking Challenge, I recruited hundreds of people to learn the strategies. I had them answer questions about how they planned to try each of the strategies, and how the implementation actually went (you can see similar exercises, so you can try answering these questions yourself in the Tactics section at the end of the book). I measured their overall time satisfaction, using my time-satisfaction scale, and how they felt about aspects of their work, both before and after the challenge. I asked people how much they agreed with various statements (on a 1-to-7-point scale) to create a workday-satisfaction scale:

* Overall, I enjoy my work.
* During my working hours, I spend time on tasks I find meaningful.
* My work matches my skills and interests.
* I have close friendships at work.
* The people I work with care about me as a person.
* During work hours, I find myself watching the clock or wishing time away.*
* I get distracted during work hours.*
* I feel anxious at the start of the workweek.*
* My workload feels manageable.
* I have a good work/life balance.
* I am exhausted at the end of the week.*
* I am good at my work.

(I scored the starred negative statements in reverse to create a consistent scale so that a higher rating meant more satisfaction at work.)

More than 85 percent of my participants worked more than 30 hours per week, with almost 35 percent claiming to work more than 40. Most were salaried, though freelancers, hourly employees, and other pay configurations were represented too. When I asked people, on a scale of 1 to 100, how likely they were to be in their current jobs a year from now, the average was 84.3. Some people even claimed 100, which I find questionable, but for the most part people weren't looking to leave their jobs. They were just interested in making their work hours better.

There was room for improvement. On the same 1-to-7-point time-satisfaction scale I used in the first chapter, people started with a score of 4.28—a little lower than some of my other surveys.

Indeed, agreement with certain statements, such as "Yesterday, I had enough time for the things I wanted to do," trended into the disagreement category (3.86 on the 1-to-7-point scale, where 4 is neutral). On the work-specific questions I asked, people reported being reasonably exhausted by the end of the workweek and were likely to get distracted during work hours.

Over the course of three weeks, I had people try out each of these strategies in turn. Without changing jobs or anything major about their lives, people were able to increase their sense of time abundance significantly during this "soft reset" (to use one respondent's words). A person who confessed to feeling rather uninspired at the beginning reported that the strategies "definitely helped me to enjoy my job more." Or as another person put it, after the challenge, she was feeling "more joy during my workday" and "less exhausted in the evening."

I think most of us would like more joy and less exhaustion. The rest of this chapter shows how my challenge participants implemented these strategies in their workdays, with ideas for how you might do that too.

Strategy #1: Spend one more hour on the work you like most

We all have some parts of our jobs we like better than others. Certainly there are parts we like less. You probably know what those are. But no doubt you have something that drew you to your job in the first place. There is probably *something* that makes you excited when you see it on your calendar, or task list for the day, or your to-do list.

What is that? Take a few minutes to make a list. It might help to look back over your calendar or planner for the last few weeks. If the first chapter inspired you to track your time, you might add a mood score (maybe on a 1 to 10 scale) next to each time block, and see where the numbers drift north. You could ask colleagues when you seem most lit up. Or you might think back to a prior job you enjoyed. What part did you find most satisfying? While there are all sorts of external benefits that can make work rewarding—I like getting paid—the deepest sense of meaning comes from being intrinsically motivated by the work itself.

I asked my Better Workday Challenge participants to think about what work they liked best. The answers ranged from reading for research to meeting with clients, interviewing and talking to sources, project planning, optimizing web texts, group problem-solving, writing, creating visuals for data visualization, SEO content planning, talking with volunteers, certain kinds of patient interactions, and other things. People described getting in a state of flow. They enjoyed a sense of discovery, of feeling that they were skilled at this type of work, and that they were doing something important.

The challenge is that in the busyness of daily life it's hard to spend as much time on the good stuff as we might like. Plenty of folks also have limited discretion over how they spend their work hours. People estimated they spent just over two and a half hours on their favorite work activity each week, though this was skewed by people who spent a lot of time on what they liked. The middle half or so was between 30 minutes and 2.5 hours per week.

I asked people to figure out how they might spend one more hour per week on this activity. This could happen as a solid hour, or 10 to 15 minutes each day. Then I asked people to figure out when they might fit in this work on a day like today, or on one of their next few workdays.

Surveying their schedules, many people decided to look for the first free block of time in the morning, understanding that time is less likely to get away from you earlier in the day. Some people identified generally open space on their calendars—for example, that Monday afternoons were often lighter. Others hoped to reduce the length of some meetings or skip optional ones. They pledged to put the favorite work activity on their to-do list or calendar.

Even though most people could figure out when they might be able to do their favorite work, they anticipated challenges. The most common one? "Fires"—that is, metaphorical ones. Many workplaces seem to have a lot of urgent things come up, whether because they're genuinely critical and time sensitive, or because of poor planning.

In any work situation where people have some autonomy, but not total autonomy, the workday becomes a series of choices of what to do with any given moment. There is a choice between the sorts of meaningful (or creative, or strategic) work that people enjoyed, and the urgent "fires" demanding attention. There is the question of whether it is better to be available for others' requests, including supervisors' requests, or whether it is better to do work that might be valuable long term but doesn't need to be done quickly. On any given day the balance can go one way or another, but people intuitively understood that shifting the balance even slightly might make a day more pleasant.

And so people developed strategies for making the good things happen. One person decided to work on a favorite activity right after lunch "because I can go into it with the mindset that it's part of my lunch"—a protected time, rather than a time subject to random fires. Others figured out ways to nudge their favorite work up the priority list, such as by offering colleagues an update on what this favorite work had accomplished, perhaps at a meeting a few days later, to get some accountability.

In other cases, the task was something intermittent, so it might not always be available, but one person decided to tell management about wanting more work like this. This is wise. Having limited space in a schedule, or limited discretion, is not the same as having no discretion. When I worked at a fast-food restaurant many years ago, it was a big win to convince my manager to let me work more shifts at the front counter (which I enjoyed) versus the drive-through (which I hated). Reasonable managers will often accommodate requests, though they might not go out of their way to offer you your favorite work. Everyone is busy. You have to be intentional about wanting to enjoy your workdays more and ask.

The good news is that, with a little nudge, people were generally able to make more time for their favorite work. In my survey at the end of the week, the mean time spent on a favorite work activity rose to about three hours, for an average increase of about 21 minutes for people who reported how much time they spent on their favorite work at both time points. While a handful of people spent 10 hours or more on their favorite work, the middle half or so fell in the range of one to three hours, which means that the majority of folks were enjoying at least some time doing this pleasant form of work.

Not surprisingly, spending more time on their favorite work tended to make people happier with their workdays. "I enjoyed work more," one man wrote—not just the favorite work, but all of it.

People experienced time in new ways:

"The week went by much faster than usual (in a good way). I left work feeling very productive."

"I felt really energized! I go into the office on Wednesdays and I felt really excited to share what I had worked on the day before. I also felt more excited to get the less exciting tasks done quickly earlier in the day."

"For the first time in a VERY LONG TIME I didn't want to stop working on Tuesday. I was having fun and I was in a flow state. I am not sure that has happened in the past two years."

Curiously, it wasn't only spending more *clock* time on their favorite work that mattered. Simply noticing that they were doing this work let people savor the experience more. "I had two very lovely visits with infant patients this week that I intentionally reminded myself to enjoy," one health-care provider reported. These babies were on the schedule anyway, but really seeing this time made the workday more pleasant.

For many people, it wasn't easy to spend more time on their favorite work. There were those fires, or the "deluge of interruptions," to use another disaster metaphor. "The lure of trying to 'clear the decks' or catch up on email was strong, mostly to reduce the worry about obligations not being met," one person reported.

"But," this person continued, "that is almost always true. I'm rarely caught up on email. I reminded myself that one to two hours of delay in responding would not matter. I'm not saving lives." Nothing was actually on fire.

I know that some people reading this might think that an hour is a small ask. What's a measly hour out of 168, or even 40? Not much, but my experience is that it doesn't take much to change a lot. If you knew you were meeting up with a dear friend for an hour over the weekend, you'd probably look forward to the weekend for quite a while. Knowing you'll be spending some time in the afternoon on an exciting project can put pep in your step all morning. You can probably find 10 to 15 minutes. One person reminded themselves that "even 10 minutes of working on it counted, and that I could at least fit that in during a busy day."

Strategy #2: Spend 15 minutes deepening a work friendship

Having close friendships at work makes work more enjoyable. Every year, Gallup reports that a positive answer to the question "Do you have a best friend at work?" is closely associated with job satisfaction. While this question reeks of the middle school cafeteria, on some level it makes sense. A best friend is someone you'd willingly spend evening and weekend hours with. These are hours that you likely would not wish away. How amazing to be able to spend time with that person while on the clock!

If you have a work best friend, excellent. But even a reasonably close acquaintance or two will do. I know that some people like to maintain separation between the workplace and their personal lives, but you need not be best friends with someone in order to feel happier in their presence. General affection is fine. Even that tends to make people feel better about the world, and any sort of affection tends to be built by spending relaxed time together. This time is cumulative, so any bit helps.

This leads to the next strategy: Spend 15 minutes each week consciously deepening a work friendship.

To do this, you first need to think of the colleagues you genuinely like. Who makes you smile? If you don't work closely with many people, or close friendships might be awkward (e.g., you're the boss of a small office), then consider people within your broader professional network (e.g., other bosses of small offices), or even fellow remote workers you see frequently at the coffee shop. Perhaps an acquaintance works in an office building near you and could meet you on breaks. Perhaps a friendly neighbor is also working from home. Choose one particular person you'd like to focus on. It might be motivational to remind yourself exactly what you like about this person, or what you have in common, such as being in the same stage of life, both being new parents, or both speaking a different first language than the one spoken at the office.

Whoever you choose, hopefully you already spend some time with this person. My participants estimated that they spent, on average, about 31 minutes per week with their chosen friend, though these estimates ranged from zero to seven hours. Sometimes people had the occasional lunch together. Sometimes they got together when they were at the same events. However, a number of people claimed they talked to this person "just in passing and before/after meetings" or "have gotten coffee or lunch but only once or twice a year." Remote workers might chat a bit on Zoom before or after meetings, but for these people, connecting was often even harder than for those who saw colleagues in person.

I had the Better Workday Challenge participants brainstorm how they might spend 15 more minutes per week with their chosen work friend. What might they engineer?

A number of people decided to reach out to schedule a coffee meetup, including a "virtual coffee" with people who weren't in the same place. People invited colleagues to go for a walk, or even decided to ask friendly questions during an online meeting and truly listen to the answers. One person suggested coworking in the same place with another remote worker, and then catching up during breaks. Others planned to ask about life when they saw the person in the hallway, though some were a bit more proactive about "randomly" bumping into people. I enjoyed this plan from an academic: "Step 1: Spy on her teaching schedule on the university website to see if we are ever there at the same time this semester (just did it: we are). Step 2: Plan to get there a little early on those days and see if we can start up a saying-hi-before-we-start-class routine." People with hybrid schedules made plans to coordinate in-the-office days with their chosen coworkers so they could meet up. One person even suggested blocking off two lunches, so if the first didn't happen due to emergencies (those fires!), the second was still an option.

After a week, they reported back. Happily, after this nudge, about two thirds of people were able to spend more time with their work friend than usual. For people estimating time spent at both points, the average increase was 37 minutes, meaning people did even better than the 15 minutes we were aiming for.

They described all sorts of wonderful moments of connection. A teacher reported going on two lunchtime walks and going out to lunch with three colleagues on a professional development day. Another person got adjoining rooms with a work friend at the annual HR conference they attended and found that "it was fun to spend a little more time chatting before we both turned in for the evening." One person talked of doing what she called "five minutes of fun" where she and a work friend would share "dumb internet memes." Another described going on a walk with a new work friend who reached out. She was nervous about how it would go, but they talked about their families and lives and it turned out to be very collegial. A person who usually met weekly with a work friend via Zoom decided to meet twice and spent more time just talking and connecting.

This challenge to spend more time with a work friend often inspired people to connect with others beyond the work friend they identified in the survey. "This week my closest friend was traveling for work, but I made a point to reach out regularly to cheer her on," one person wrote. "Aside from her, I made a point to linger in conversations and intentionally reach out to others in an effort to connect."

People found that actively spending more time with friends did, in fact, correspond with feeling happier at work. One person shared that "I ended the week in a much better mood than usual, despite weather hazards and power outages." Time started to feel different. "The days I spent a little extra time with work friends seemed to go faster than usual and I felt happier when I left work for the day with a better sense of satisfaction and accomplishment," one person reported. When work seems to go faster there's no need to wish time away.

To be sure, this strategy didn't always work. One man noted that he tried to drop by a colleague's office, but this person decided not to come in that day. "Okay, I was sad. Prepandemic I had friends in the office. Since then, they've been working from home and I don't see them in the office. I've not put out the effort to find new work friends," he said. There are many benefits of remote and hybrid work, but they do require more effort to maintain casual connections. You might reach out to colleagues to check which days they will be in the office in person and try to match their schedules. If you're mostly remote, you can go to any in-person opportunities that are available, and try to schedule a few casual, virtual chats with colleagues who seem friendly before or after meetings or when you'd normally be taking a break. If you've been lax on this, try to be patient with the process, but don't give up prematurely. It's the rare organization where no one wants to be friendly. Spending an extra 15 minutes a week over baseline, week after week, working to build friendships will result in something.

I know that not everyone is a social butterfly. A number of people confessed that this strategy brought up feelings of vulnerability about reaching out to colleagues. As one person put it, "It's awkward to ask 'Will you be my friend?' (not literally, but you're still putting yourself out there in asking)." Some wondered this: If you have convinced someone to meet you for coffee, or even if you both just get to a meeting early in order to chat, what do you talk about?

Small talk isn't natural for everyone. If you struggle on this front, here's a practical suggestion: "I find that Mondays are the easiest days to build work friendships because we can chat about the weekend," one participant shared. You can always start a conversation in the break room, or before a meeting on Monday, by asking how people spent the previous weekend. You can also ask on Thursday or Friday what plans people have coming up the next weekend. Your own plans can serve as a conversational starting point if your friendlier colleagues bring up this topic with you. People might be nicer than you think. One person who'd been feeling isolated shared that it was a struggle to speak with people, but "doing the challenge helped me feel better mentally and reconnecting with people made me feel better about myself and helped me realize I have people who care." Or as one person put it, "I felt more connected and warmer where there had been coldness and aloofness."

Strategy #3: Take two intentional breaks each day

The final leg of the workday triangle is autonomy. People have highly variable amounts of autonomy in their actual jobs, but almost everyone has some autonomy over the time during working hours when they are not working—that is, when they are taking breaks.

In some jobs these are formal and built into the rhythm of the day. Breaks might be more ad hoc in other jobs, but almost everyone takes at least short breaks during the workday, if for no other reason than that people need to use the restroom. There's reasonable evidence that breaks reduce fatigue and boost energy. One meta-analysis of 22 studies, involving thousands of participants, found that taking mere "microbreaks" (up to 10 minutes) was associated with reduced fatigue and increased "vigor" (to use the researchers' term).

The trouble is, particularly in information jobs, that people don't always take their breaks consciously. You've been working on a project, and you see your inbox is filling up, so you look at it, and after answering a colleague's query, you see a breaking news headline, so you click over to read the story. While at that news site, you read a report about a player on your fantasy football roster. You pick up your phone to text a friend who's in your league, and then see that the WhatsApp list for your kid's soccer team is lighting up because someone (you know who) is complaining that the kids' snacks have all been too sugary this week. You're about to weigh in with your feelings on Capri-Sun when you realize you need to get back to your project before your next meeting. That was a break, but it didn't feel relaxing. Since you never got off the devices you use to work, you may have felt like you never stopped working. You might not even acknowledge that you took a break—which can contribute to a story of having no time.

I saw this in the responses to the Better Workday Challenge. I asked people whether they regularly took breaks, and I got answers such as "I didn't take any breaks yesterday—I don't typically end up having any breaks other than periodic scrolling of email newsletters some days (five minutes here and there)." But those are, in fact, breaks. And even in jobs where breaks are more obvious—such as in a factory or restaurant, where you might clock out or your manager might tell you to go take your break—people don't always think through what would maximize rejuvenation. Reading a mystery novel for 15 minutes on a break in your shift, or calling a friend, might be more fun than looking at Instagram influencers. But the latter is likely easier in the moment.

Taking intentional breaks means consciously replacing these low-value breaks with higher-value leisure. If you're going to take a break anyway, it may as well be restorative. Taking two intentional breaks each day means that even if you don't like any-thing else about your job, you'll be able to reclaim 20 minutes or more each day for yourself. It's like a mini vacation.

I asked my challenge participants to brainstorm activities they could do during a 10-minute break from work (generally in addition to any longer meal breaks they might take, though one could tag on an activity to a longer break too). People came up with the usual (grab a cup of coffee, go for a quick walk), and some more interesting ideas, such as going up and down the stairs ("my office is on the sixth floor"), using the restroom on another floor, feeding the birds when at home or puttering in the garden, lying in a hammock, throwing a ball with the dog, writing in a gratitude journal, popping over to the supermarket next door, reading a book or some favorite Substack newsletters, paging through a cookbook, listening to a short podcast, looking at photos, doodling, crocheting, coloring, doing the various *New York Times* games or an online puzzle, texting or calling friends, writing a note, welcoming family members home from school during a midafternoon break, playing with Legos, or solving a Rubik's Cube.

I invited people to choose two activities for their breaks on the day they were taking my survey, or for the next workday. Curiously, even without my prompting them to, a lot of people chose two different activities, thus constructing a break "portfo-lio" for each day. You do a puzzle for 10 minutes in the morning and take a 15-minute walk in the afternoon. Or you read a novel for 10 minutes in the morning and go sit outside with a cup of tea in midafternoon—a level of variety that can make life feel more fun, and that might not happen without some intention.

I had them strategize how they might fit these breaks into the day, or at least remember to pause to take the breaks. People pondered if they might end back-to-back meetings early, or if it might be possible to take a five-minute walk between seeing patients (or a longer one if there was a no-show). They thought through challenges, such as feeling self-conscious about visibly taking breaks when coworkers complained of being too busy. One person vowed to "set an alarm and let my colleague know 'I am just having a short break and I will get back to you with a clear head afterward.'" They worried about getting sucked into unintentional breaks (nonwork email, scrolling) and then not having time for good stuff.

Not everyone took breaks. And even for those who were somewhat successful with taking breaks, life happened, such as the usual challenges of meetings running late, people stopping by the office, or "the 'just-one-more-thing' situation where I'm 'just going to finish this email quick and then I'm going to take my break' . . . and then I forget about the break until it's time for me to hop on my next meeting." There was inertia: "I wanted to get outside and take a walk, but in the office it feels like the two-elevator process isn't worth it."

But when people did take intentional breaks, they generally saw results. For those reporting on their breaks before and after this week's strategy, agreement with the statements "My work breaks boosted my energy levels" and "My work breaks boosted my mood" rose by more than 10 percent over the course of the week. In other words, people's breaks were getting better at doing what a break is supposed to do.

As their work breaks got better, my participants reported all sorts of lovely experiences. People got outside to enjoy nature, in many cases enjoying walks in beautiful fall weather. Others folded in time for their personal priorities, such as taking an extended break to go watch an event at the kids' school. One participant stopped by the library; another went for a 20-minute run. Some prioritized real leisure, such as walking with a friend to a local cake stall. While some people resorted to subterfuge ("printing ebooks . . . gives me the joy of nonscreen reading, without the guilt of holding a novel or fun book while at work"), one person brazenly sat in the office kitchen with a cup of coffee and a physical book. Others used their time, even small bits of time, to infuse some quiet and stillness into a busy workday. One person went to Mass, which is not necessarily the world's shortest break, but doable over lunch. One person celebrated handing in a project by "walking over to Pinkberry, ordering my favorite fall flavors, and eating the whole thing without distraction and in deep, quiet appreciation." People meditated and practiced deep breathing while waiting for the copy machine to finish.

These breaks made people more cheerful and often more productive. As one person put it, "I was having trouble finding the words I wanted to use while writing a grant application. I went for a walk and when I came back, the words seemed to magically appear!" Another person noted feeling calmer and less easily rattled by coworkers and Slack messages after an intentional break. People talked of being happier at the end of the day, and of feeling less stressed. Even when folks had been taking breaks before, they noted that it felt different to have 10 dedicated minutes to relax fully versus a constant distracted scrolling.

Some participants reported that taking real breaks resulted in less distracted work the rest of the time. "I've experienced a sense of peace and lightness during the workday as the result of mental focus and not being pulled away," one person reported, and "by Friday I was able to take proper breaks without feeling anxious or guilty about being away from my desk. I went outside with the dogs to play fetch and later read a chapter of a novel outside on what may be the last day that's possible (I live in Nova Scotia)."

While the breaks themselves were fun, some people noted that anticipating the breaks made work feel better for a lot longer than the breaks themselves. One person recounted being in a better mood for hours because she kept thinking, "Ooo, I get to take a break today and have a chai latte." Knowing something good is coming up, like listening to a funny podcast, or reading the next chapter in an exciting book, can make even a dreary staff meeting a little more pleasant. Looking forward to something is pretty much the opposite of wishing time away. If two well-chosen 10-minute breaks can make that happen, that is a solid return on investment.

Stop wishing time away

As my Better Workday Challenge participants tried to make their workdays better, they became more satisfied with their time. Scores on the overall time-satisfaction scale and the workday satisfaction subscale rose to a statistically significant degree over the course of three weeks. Some of the biggest leaps came on the statements "Yesterday I had enough time for the things I wanted to do" (up 24 percent) and "Yesterday I did not waste time on the things that weren't important to me" (up 19 percent). People reported being less distracted (a 12 percent change) and less exhausted (an 8 percent change). Agreement scores with the statement "Overall, I'm making progress on my professional goals" rose 12 percent, and agreement with the statement "Overall, I feel good about my relationships and my progress on my personal priorities" rose 17 percent.

As with any challenge, some people followed the directions more closely than others. I asked people the extent to which they implemented each of the strategies (on a 7-point scale from "Not at all" to "Completely"). Of the people who implemented all three strategies at least "Somewhat" (4 on the 7-point scale), their average increase in time satisfaction was 0.90 points, compared with 0.67 points for everyone in the analysis sample, and their average increase in workday satisfaction was 0.31 points, compared with 0.17 points for everyone in the analysis sample. For the people who implemented all three strategies at least "A good bit" (5 on the 7-point scale), the average increase in time satisfaction and workday satisfaction were 0.97 points and 0.46 points respectively.

In other words, people who implemented these strategies more faithfully tended to see more results. That doesn't necessarily mean anything on its own. It could be that the people who implemented the strategies more faithfully were the people for whom the strategies felt most relevant, which is why they were able to benefit from them. However, it is also possible that those who didn't implement the strategies might have seen more results if they had.

In any case, I could see effects in people's qualitative answers. "I started this challenge in a place where I am seriously considering leaving my current job," one person wrote. "These strategies helped me to realize that there are still things within my control that I can do to make my experience better, regardless of whether I choose to stay."

This sense of agency is exactly what I'm going for. People wind up in jobs for all sorts of reasons, and then stay for all sorts of reasons too. Sometimes a job is, mostly, a paycheck. But whatever the circumstances, there is almost always something we can do to make our day-to-day experience of life better. "All three strategies, when implemented, made me feel like I had more control over my work time and my experience of working," one person wrote. "In general, it made my work seem more positive and vibrant, and something I could look forward to."

This positivity had spillover effects for the rest of life. "I had more energy for activities after work," one more seasoned employee said, as work started to feel more meaningful. "I was actually starting to mentor younger employees, rather than just trying to keep up during the day."

While none of these strategies required much time, I did ask busy people to make space in their schedules for something else. The good news is that I know from long experience that putting more meaningful things into life often crowds out less important matters. If you're meeting a work friend for coffee in fifteen minutes, or you're deeply absorbed in whatever topic drew you to your job in the first place, you might spend less time cleaning out your inbox. That might not be a bad thing. One person wrote of needing to be more careful with the schedule when planning out the week, in order to fit in time for meaningful work, friendships, and breaks, but "this had the delightful side effect of [my] feeling more organized throughout the week, and being more aware of where I had flex in my schedule."

People had long-term plans for continuing with these strategies at least to some degree. An educator with a fairly inflexible schedule planned to implement these strategies "in a modified way that makes sense for me: one 10-minute break per day [plus] taking an actual lunch break, rather than working through lunch; dedicating one 45-minute prep block per week to focus on work I enjoy doing; continuing to eat lunch with my colleagues every Friday."

Another person wrote that "I am already planning to schedule the meetings I own for 45 to 50 minutes to allow for breaks for myself and my team."

When I followed up a month later, I found that time satisfaction scores stayed elevated, and in many cases continued to rise. For the 122 people who filled out the one month follow-up survey, agreement scores for the statement "Yesterday, I had enough time for the things I wanted to do" rose 30 percent from the pre-challenge survey. Agreement with the statement "Yesterday, I did not waste time on things that weren't important to me" was up 31 percent.

"I have a better sense of how to turn a blah workday or workweek around," one person reported. "I might not use all three strategies every day, but if I use at least one of them every day, work feels pretty good."

Even in stressful situations, people felt more agency. "There will ALWAYS be too much to do," one person wrote. "There isn't some mystical, mythical time in the future when it will all be done. And even if there were, then what? Am I really going to wish away my whole life waiting for someday that really may never come?" Better to "enjoy life now, and while I may not love every task that comes across my desk, I can deal with it."

Plenty of people will never be truly in love with their work hours, but aiming for better is possible. In the vastness of time, it may require shifting fewer hours than you think.

CHAPTER 5

EMBRACE YOUR GOLDEN HOURS

On a September day not long ago, I got a note from a woman I'll call Rebecca. She had changed jobs in August, and while she was doing a different sort of work, she was still working for the same group of companies. The volume of work itself had not shifted much.

But how she felt about her time after work had shifted a great deal, which was why she was reaching out to me.

"Before I changed jobs, I found it very challenging to leave work before 5:30 p.m.," she said. The executive team would often assign work later in the day, and she felt pressed to complete it before getting out the door. Her commute home was about an hour. That meant that she'd arrive back at the house around 6:30 p.m. "I always felt rushed and anxious that I wasn't home with the kids at a reasonable time," she wrote. "I found my commute very stressful, especially when sitting in traffic," which was the norm for the first part of her commute. As a result, when she got home she felt like the evening was mostly over. It was too late and she was too spent to accomplish much before bedtime.

Workdays at her new job ended with a different vibe. Her

team wrapped up around 5:00 p.m., which meant everyone was out in the parking lot by 5:15 p.m. She still had to face down the hour-long commute, though, and she was still in the same traffic, meaning she arrived home at approximately 6:15 p.m.

Alert observers will note that this is . . . not much earlier. And yet "it feels so different," she told me. "That different approach and 15-minute change has made me feel so much more relaxed on my commute." Now, "I'm not anxious in traffic and I feel like I have most of the 6 o'clock hour for my personal responsibilities." With this newfound sense of time abundance, "I even rearranged patio furniture so I can sit on the porch outside the kitchen with the dogs for a few minutes each night enjoying the sunset."

Rebecca and I emailed back and forth trying to understand what was going on. Perhaps she felt guilty about leaving her previous job at 5:30 p.m., since others were still there, and those bad feelings affected her leisure and family time. Or "it could be the perception of the six o'clock hour being available to me," she suggested—that 6:15 p.m. rounds to 6:00, but 6:30 p.m. rounds to 7:00. Still, that seemed like a bit of a stretch. "So it is clearly mindset," she noted, even if she was not entirely sure why.

What was clear was this: Though the amount of time available hadn't changed much, she had begun to see evenings differently. For whatever reason, now they felt like a real time of day, available for her to choose how to spend. As the seasons changed, she was watching the golden light on the trees and fields near her Pennsylvania home. She was starting to appreciate the possibilities and pondering what she might do.

❋

I FIND REBECCA'S REVELATION INTERESTING BECAUSE I THINK THE way she experienced evenings in her first job is common. For many people, weekday evenings are an afterthought in their lives. People are tired after a long day and a long commute. For some, like Rebecca, stress means the time feels too small to be usable—forgettable scraps after everything else is dealt with. For others, evenings become a grinding second shift of doing all the housework that didn't get done while everyone was at work and school, or a battle to get everyone fed, bathed, and into bed. For still others, evenings disappear into mindless screen time that can run late enough to steal momentum from the next day.

But as I study evenings, I see that this is a lot of time to simply write off as the leftovers after work. The day is not over after dinner. Part of recognizing the bigness of time is seeing this. Someone arriving home from work at 6:30 p.m. and going to bed at 10:30 p.m. has four hours each night, Monday to Thursday, to play with. That's 16 hours, which is the equivalent of two workdays. Getting home at 6:15 p.m. changes this to 17 hours—a nice bonus—but a tweak that is hardly transformative in itself.

What is transformative is how one chooses to view this time.

In our quest to fall in love with our schedules, I believe the key to enjoying this time more is to get that same mindset shift toward abundance that Rebecca experienced, even without changing jobs. I believe that with a few simple changes, evening hours can feel more expansive and pleasant. These changes are accessible even to people who work long hours, or who have long commutes, or who are chasing after toddlers, or shuttling kids to basketball practice, or all of the above.

Just as retirees might celebrate their "golden years" of leisure and family time after decades of work, I think we can celebrate our "golden hours" every evening—truly enjoying this family and personal time after our paid labors are done. I have seen evenings transform into golden hours for hundreds of people adopting these changes. I believe they can change for you too.

No reason to be miserable

I came up with this "golden hours" reframing because I personally have struggled with my evenings. For many years, my evenings were largely about getting lots of small kids to bed, many times on my own. Then they were about shuttling older kids to activities *and* getting small kids to bed, though slightly less on my own (my ability to be in two places at once being limited). My kids have never been great sleepers; bedtime has been contentious. Let's just say it hasn't been my favorite time of day.

But I track my time, and so I know that I have never spent all the hours after work and before bed convincing small people to stay in their beds. I have noticed that when I think about what I'd like to do during my evenings, and figure out how to implement at least one limited golden-hour intention, I have a high probability of following through. When I do, I am more likely to enjoy myself.

We are not talking anything big here. The magic formula for enjoying evening hours more is this:

Understand the landscape. Get a good sense of what your evenings look like.

Set (small) intentions. Set one intention each day of something you want to do for 30 to 60 minutes beyond work, housework, or the physical care of family members. Figure out where this can go.

Notice and savor. As you are doing your golden-hour activity, notice how it feels and try to appreciate it, with the goal of increasing enjoyment over time.

For me an intention might mean 30 minutes of doing a puzzle, or sitting on the hammock with a magazine, or getting my little ones out in the pool on a summer evening. Even if there is not much time, there is usually some time. Desires can exist alongside requirements. I can read for 30 minutes before bed at night even if I am facing down deadlines, and supervising showers and room cleanup. I can spend 30 minutes working on a puzzle while my youngest is watching a video, and I can notice that this leisure time is happening. There is no reason to be miserable. There is no reason to feel like this time doesn't exist.

I have found this mindset shift so helpful that I decided to test what would happen when lots of people began setting small evening intentions. Over the course of a week, would they start to enjoy their time more too? What about a month later—would any of these good habits stick?

The answer is yes. It turns out that even busy people—and even people who are already satisfied with their time—can take their days from good to better by paying attention to time that might be easy to overlook.

How to transform your evenings

In the summer of 2024, 179 people participated in what I called the Evening Hours Challenge. Of these, more than 90 percent worked for pay, and more than 70 percent had kids at home. As with the Time Tracking Challenge and the Better Workday Challenge, I had them answer questions to determine how satisfied they were with their time. I also created an evening-satisfaction scale, and had people register their disagreement or agreement with a few statements on a 7-point scale:

- Overall, I feel good about how I spend my evening hours.
- In the evenings, I find myself wishing time away, or counting hours until bedtime.*
- I don't have as much time for myself as I'd like in the evening.*
- I stay up later than I'd like in order to have free time.*
- I spend a lot of time in the evenings on chores or family responsibilities.*
- I don't have enough time to complete all my chores or to-dos in the evening before my intended bedtime.*
- Evenings are my favorite part of the day.
- In the evenings, I have meaningful time with family and/or friends.
- In the evenings, I pursue my hobbies and interests.

(As with the Better Workday Challenge, I scored the starred negative statements in reverse to create a consistent scale so a higher rating meant more satisfaction in the evening.)

As with the Time Tracking Challenge and the Better Workday Challenge, people on average started out more satisfied with their time than unsatisfied with their time. At the beginning of the week, the overall time satisfaction score for this group was a 4.52 on the 1-to-7-point scale, and their evening satisfaction score was 4.03 on the 1-to-7-point scale. I then introduced people to the three-step approach to improving evenings.

1. Understand the landscape

For many people, weekday evenings are such an afterthought that they don't have any sense of where the time goes, or even how much time there is. Even people who have clear morning routines, or who have a good grasp on their work hours, can struggle to describe their evenings. To be sure, that's sometimes because evenings themselves can vary in length and tend to be less regimented than the mornings. People might work later some days than others, or have more commitments on some nights. And while many adults wake up at set times for work or family responsibilities, they're far less likely to have a set bedtime (though you should set a bedtime; I'll talk more about that later in the chapter).

That said, even if evenings don't all look the same, it's possible to get a sense of the landscape. If you try tracking your time for a week, pay special attention to your post-work, pre-bed hours. If you don't want to track all 168 hours of the week, try logging just your evening hours for a few days to see what you see. How much space is available? What has to happen? What doesn't? What's working well? What do you wish could be different?

I asked the Evening Hours Challenge participants about their schedules. The vast majority of people finished work before 6:00 p.m., and many finished at 5:00 p.m. or even earlier, which is consistent with general data from the American Time Use Survey. The bulk of people also went to bed after 10:00 p.m., meaning that the average weekday evening was more than five hours long. Even if small bits of work, such as email checking, did punctuate this time, from a numerical perspective, there was a lot of time to play around with.

I asked people what they liked and didn't like about their evenings. Some folks felt all right with them. People liked the possibility of relaxing, and of spending time with family, but many shared my general impression that this time of day is hard to use well. Even those who were satisfied with their evenings seldom had a particular focus to their evenings, beyond the have-to-dos. And those with lower initial scores were sometimes quite rueful about the time. When I asked what people liked most about their evenings, one person replied, "I've literally never thought about this question. I only ever think about how unhappy I am with how I spend my time. I honestly can't even think of anything positive to say."

So there was a lot to work with here.

In general, the complaints fell in a few categories. Unsurprisingly, many people noted their overall fatigue. "I feel tired from a full workday [so] I don't feel motivated to do much for myself or anyone else," one person wrote. "After I put the kids to bed I just get sucked into doomscrolling." Another noted that "I'm an early riser, so I often feel like I just collapse into bed instead of having a routine." And as one person memorably put it, "I am out of energy and often out of sorts by the time evening rolls around."

People with young kids noted the volume of things that had to happen after work and before lights out. One educator reported that he often needed to grade assignments at night, and so weekday evenings felt crunched as he tried to do household tasks, help his kid with homework, and catch up on what he hadn't been able to finish at work. One woman who spent evenings driving children to sports wrote that meals felt chaotic, and that she often worked in the car while her kids were at practice because she'd left early from work in order to get them out the door. Once everyone was home there might be lengthy bedtime battles; one parent, invoking Sisyphus, recounted "the feeling that I am pushing a rock uphill trying to get everyone to go to bed." To get relaxed, autonomous time, parents sometimes bargained down how much sleep they needed: "My ideal bedtime is not that much after my toddlers and so I often stay up later than I would like to fit in me-time."

Others, however, complained of the time feeling more nebulous. One person lamented that "somehow at least an hour disappears into smoke and suddenly it's 10:30 p.m. and I haven't done what I intended to do." Electronic entertainment of various forms played a role here. One person bemoaning the TV tallies said, "I enjoy some of what we watch, but often look back on that time and feel 'I just lost five hours of my life, never to get it back.'" Another person was well aware that she had more available space than her peers with families, but she still struggled to do anything all that enjoyable: "I definitely waste all that free time," she wrote.

The good news: awareness is the first step. Because when we know what evenings really look like, we can start to see what might be possible.

2. Set (small) intentions

People's nightly obligations and experiences of weekday evenings vary. But from studying thousands of time logs over the years, I can tell you that almost everyone has some available time, and some discretion over how to use it, even if there are limits on this autonomy. Someone solo parenting three small children might not be able to leave the house easily. Someone whose work shifts end unpredictably might have trouble making time-specific plans. Or something urgent might come up with work at night that must be dealt with before the morning. But even within constraints it is often possible to do *something* enjoyable.

So once you have a sense of your evening landscape, take some time to dream up a handful of enjoyable evening intentions. What could you do for 30 to 60 minutes? What would you genuinely look forward to?

I asked my Evening Hours Challenge participants to brainstorm intentions, and they came up with all sorts of ideas.

By far the most popular intention was reading, with a

number of participants specifying that they wanted to read "uninterrupted."

Since it was summer when I did the challenge, some also wanted to enjoy time outside, suggesting things such as "Spend time on the front porch watching fireflies with a cup of tea," or "Sit on the patio while the kids play," or "more time in the pool," or even looking at the stars.

Numerous people mentioned the possibility of exercise, like taking a family walk, or going to the gym.

Others wanted to connect with those close to them, listing activities such as "Play with my daughter outside on the driveway," "Go-karts with the family," "Board games with family" "Lego with 9-y-o after 4-y-o is asleep," or even "Do dinner with another family." Some planned to call or FaceTime friends or family members, or get a drink with a friend.

There were hobby intentions such as practicing the flute, baking something easy, or creating a scrapbook layout.

Some people wanted to go out for ice cream or a special dessert.

Some participants did mention screens, though the "intention" part nudged more thought than the usual routine of scrolling through Netflix. A handful of people suggested watching a movie as a weekday intention, which is certainly doable if your evening is four to five hours long. One man set an intention to play a particular video game with his wife and kids.

I instructed people to think about when they might do these activities and to make a plan. Those who wanted to get together with friends needed to check in with those friends about their availability. Some folks needed to look at the weather; a bike ride to get Slurpees at 7-Eleven might not work so well in a thunderstorm. One woman made a plan to walk during a child's sports practice (it's an excellent idea in general to use this time for personal pursuits; another parent shared that she was part of a book club that met during her kid's swim practice!). I encouraged people who chose an intention like reading, which could theoretically be done at any point, to choose a specific contingent or clock time to hold themselves accountable. Setting an intention such as "I will read my book for 45 minutes on Tuesday night after the kids go to bed, and for 30 minutes while they are at gymnastics practice on Wednesday evening" vastly increases the chances that this happens versus just saying "I'm going to read more."

I asked people to anticipate challenges and how they might address them. People worried about fatigue, but they had their strategies. One woman suggested that she "at least try for 15 minutes and give myself the option to quit if I don't have the energy." Another person noted "accepting that 20 minutes is infinitely better than zero," and that to keep things interesting, one might rotate through preferred activities.

Others needed to work through logistical challenges. One woman who wanted to read more noted that drawn-out toddler bedtimes tended to cut into her reading time, but she could still listen to an audiobook (via headphones) while sitting in the kids' rooms. A person who wanted to relax on the patio noted that this "requires it not to be raining, or have recently rained, and it's been raining a lot lately!" But it would be possible to set a backup slot: Monday and Tuesday could both be potential porch nights, and if it rained Monday, Tuesday might still be an option.

Others needed to resist the lure of effortless fun. A person who wanted to create art noted that "I can do pretty much anything any day which often leads to 'nothing, every day.'" In the moment, Netflix was often more tempting, but this person decided to make various art materials available and visible to lower the perceived transaction costs.

Whatever the intention, I encouraged people to decide ahead of time, so they could manage their energy. If you wait until you get home from work at 6:30 p.m. to decide what you want to do in the evening, the answer is going to be "nothing." You won't have the energy to make a plan.

On the other hand, if you know you're going to play a board game at 7:30 with your partner and the neighbors, you create a mental picture of your day with that coming up. You don't exhaust yourself unnecessarily, or work late if you don't need to. You might even be more productive during the day to ward off the need to do scattered work tasks at night. Someone decided to hold herself accountable to her intentions by posting a list on the wall by her work computer, and then taking a moment to contemplate the list before shutting down for the day. Another person adopted this strategy to increase the odds of the intentions happening: "I will set an alarm and have them listed on the whiteboard in the kitchen." Even folks with screen-time intentions mentioned the value of choosing ahead of time. If you spend 30 or more minutes puttering around the kitchen while deciding what movie to watch, even if you reach a decision that your spouse doesn't resent, you won't be able to get through a two-hour movie after an 8:00 p.m. kid bedtime if you need the lights off at 10:30 p.m. But if you know by quitting time which two-hour movie you're watching, you can both look forward to it, and have it ready to go, and be done in time to wind down.

Some people needed to compress housework, or ask for help (e.g., each partner takes the kids one night each week, so each parent can also go out one night a week). I know that another general challenge is that some people assume they need to go along with the flow of the household, and see what everyone else is doing first. This isn't a bad thing; parents of teenagers might linger in the kitchen to see if they want to talk, and if your spouse has evening intentions, that's good to know. But if that's your only guiding principle for time, this can mean that a lot of nights are spent aimlessly. For anyone trying to reconcile this, remember that a small intention doesn't need to be a heavy lift. We are only talking a few 30- to 60-minute intentions a week. If you've got 16 or more golden hours Monday to Thursday, that still leaves plenty of time for seeing how life unfolds.

3. Notice and savor

As you start putting these 30- to 60-minute intentions into your golden hours, be sure to notice how this feels. What does a week feel like if you go to the gym one night, meet up with the neighbors for takeout on another night, and read a mystery novel (your favorite genre!) for 30 minutes before bed most days? How does time change if you do a puzzle with your spouse after the kids go to bed one night, and take the kids to an ice cream social at a community center some night? While you are doing these things you can pause and try to savor the experience. You can cement the memories and the good feelings by pondering how you might describe these experiences to someone else. You could take pictures or record these bits of pleasure in a journal.

The good news is that most people in the Evening Hours Challenge were successful in making their intentions happen. At the end of the week, more than three quarters of people agreed at least somewhat that they had been able to make space for their intentions.

People's time-satisfaction scores had also risen by a statistically significant amount. Scores on the overall time-satisfaction scale rose by about 12 percent. There were particularly pronounced increases in the statements "Yesterday, I had enough time for the things I wanted to do" (17 percent) and "Yesterday,

I did not waste time on things that weren't important to me" (23 percent).

Curiously, agreement with the statement "Yesterday, I got enough sleep to feel well rested" rose 19 percent. While the Evening Hours Challenge wasn't about getting to bed on time, I suspect participants felt more rested because when people started thinking through their evenings and setting intentions, they were able to plan in me-time before the wee hours. Leisure time and sleep were no longer at odds. Indeed, agreement with the statement "I stay up later than I'd like in order to have free time" decreased significantly by the end of the week.

Scores on the entire evening-satisfaction scale rose by about 12 percent. There was a particularly notable rise—29 percent—in agreement with the statement "Overall, I feel good about how I spend my evening hours."

These changes showed up in people's free-form responses. Among the victories:

"It was super calming to take an hour to read uninterrupted."

"I really enjoyed hiking/walking with my family after dinner twice this week and was encouraged to leave the house because of this challenge. It broke up the evening task list of feeding everyone and cleaning up."

"I did yoga on Monday. I didn't really feel like it, but I was proud I did an activity instead of scrolling/watching another episode of TV. And afterward I felt better."

"Finding time with friends is always a struggle, scheduling-wise, but we were able to pull it off! It gave me something to look forward to during the week and a sense of accomplishment heading into the weekend."

As people put more fun things into their lives, time felt different.

"The week flew by and I didn't feel like it was a drag."

"After setting aside some time for my own pursuits, I felt more relaxed and able to connect with my family."

"I ran twice . . . I also took a Pilates class twice. Both gave me something to look forward to after work and made the evening feel long, in a good way."

"I was looking forward to my Monday-night plans (drink with a friend) all day. That improved the start of my week."

"I was shocked that I had time to do these things and that there was still plenty of time for everything else."

To be sure, some people were not able to get to their intentions. Things came up. A parent whose children went on something of a sleep strike lost the motivation for anything beyond basic survival. A man lamented that he just didn't have enough energy for music practice "between household duties, the kid, the dog. It just got pushed aside." Someone reported that they were "still struggling with how unscheduled my partner tends to be and how tough it is to line up my need for structure with their looser approach to the evenings."

Interestingly, one challenge that came up was that some people *already* had a lot scheduled for their evenings, including fun things, and thus they weren't able to fit more fun things in. If that sounds like you, consider this: Enjoying your golden hours might be about noticing the time that is already there. If you are taking a nice long walk with the dog where you chat with the neighbors, and you read a good book for 30 minutes before bed, you probably don't need to also watch a movie or go get a Slurpee. Just savor these things as you are doing them.

Given the realities of life, many people did wind up modifying their intentions. For example, if you set an intention to go on an hour-long trail run, that might become a 30-minute one if a work meeting runs late. But that can still be nice. One person had planned a family walk, but the whole family didn't want to walk, so this intention switched to spending one-on-one time with the kid who did want to go. Some folks realized it was fine to simplify the rest of life to make it all work: "[I] was okay having frozen pizza for dinner in order to use dinner prep time to bike ride."

These happy golden hours

My Evening Hours Challenge participants saw a lot of boosted life satisfaction in a week. And it seemed to last, as many people were still implementing these strategies a month later and deriving roughly the same amount of satisfaction from them. For the more than 100 people who answered my follow-up survey a month later, the average score on the time-satisfaction scale rose from 4.67 at the beginning of the project to 5.17 at the end of the week, and was about the same a month later. The average score on the evening-satisfaction scale for this group was 4.15 at the beginning of the project, and 4.64 at the end of the week, and was also about the same a month later. For the statement "Overall, I feel good about how I spend my evening hours," scores rose from 4.18 at the beginning to 5.35 at the end of the week, and were still at 5.11 a month later. Particularly gratifying to me was that at the one-month mark, nearly 9 out of 10 people expressed some level of disagreement with the statement

"In the evenings, I find myself wishing time away, or counting hours until bedtime." All time is precious, so the less time we wish away, the better.

Since the Evening Hours Challenge participants saw benefits by setting a few simple intentions, I believe you will too. As you think about your golden hours, here are a few more strategies that can help you relish this time.

1. Set a bedtime

Most of us understand that a day has a beginning. We're a little less sold on the idea that each day has an end. But it does. Having a set bedtime can not only help you get enough sleep, it can give your entire evening shape. You know the dimensions of your golden hours, and within those dimensions you can make wiser choices.

So figure out when you need to wake up. Figure out how much sleep you need. Most adults need somewhere between seven and eight hours; if you track your time for a few weeks you will likely see an overall average that's somewhere in there. Count back this number of hours from your wake-up time, and you will discover your bedtime. So if you need to wake up at 6:30 a.m., and you need 7.5 hours of sleep, your bedtime is 11:00 p.m. Set some sort of reminder for 30 minutes before this time to nudge you to wind down, and life will start feeling a lot more orderly.

2. Try TOAD time

Fresh air is a known mood booster, so consider taking some of your evening intentions outside. In my household, the littler kids like to do "time outside after dinner," aka TOAD time (if the double "time" with that acronym bothers you, call it "together outside after dinner"). At least during the seven months of the year when it's light until 7:00 p.m., it's possible to get outside in the evening and do something. It could be playing on the swing set, or riding bikes, or hacking away at the brush in the backyard, but everyone seems to be happier outside, including the supervising adult. If you don't have little kids, you might sit around a fire pit or go hang out on the neighbors' porch, or buy a headlamp and go for a walk. Being outside after dinner feels like bonus time. It's a reminder that the day isn't actually over. You can fit in a lot.

3. Have a little adventure

Routines are great, but too much sameness makes time forgettable. Little adventures shake things up. So, one night a week, perhaps as one of your evening intentions, aim to go somewhere and do something that's a bit more memorable. You could bike to a bookstore or library with evening hours, or go to an industry happy hour. Take the kids to a new playground or get dinner from a food truck. You can still change into your pajamas straight after coming home from work every other night, but sometimes it's nice to have an answer for how this night is different from all the others.

4. Take one night for you

Everyone deserves to be interested in his or her own life. You can completely transform your golden hours by taking one night a week for your own passions. You might join a softball team that plays on Tuesdays, or meet up with friends every Wednesday night to run, or tutor English language learners at the community center on Monday nights. While you can do whatever you want on your night "off" from chores or caregiving, I would suggest doing something that involves a commitment to other people. If you just decide to see what you feel like doing, these plans can fall apart when you're tired, or work feels busy, or someone needs you to drive them somewhere. If your spouse's train is late, you won't text a sitter or call in a favor from a friend to watch your kids if you don't have somewhere you actually have to be. And so, frequently, you won't get your night off. But if you play in a string quartet that meets every Wednesday at 7:00 p.m., if you don't show up, they are a string trio. A commitment makes your fun rise up the hierarchy in your schedule. You will do it, and then you will reap the benefits of this active self-care.

5. Do effortful fun

People often tell me they would love to read more, or do hobbies such as sketching or needlework, if only they had the time! Yet many of us do find time for our electronic hobbies of reading headlines, half-heartedly checking email, and following up on social media comments. This digital leisure is "effortless" in the sense of not requiring much planning or energy. "Effortful" fun, such as reading a book, or calling a friend, demands more of the participant. So it's always easier to opt for the effortless variety.

It makes sense, but you can create a better leisure balance by making effortful fun a little easier—such as by downloading the Kindle app to your phone, or leaving your puzzle accessible, or putting your hobby supplies where you'd normally watch TV— and then challenging yourself to do a little bit of effortful fun *first*. If you find yourself pulling out your phone to peruse YouTube videos, read an ebook for three minutes before you visit the app.

Most likely, you'll keep reading the book because effortful fun is, in fact, fun, once you overcome the initial resistance. But even if you read for just a few minutes and then switch over, you'll still have gotten to do both kinds of fun, which is an improvement.

Insist on pleasure

It's easy to tell ourselves stories of having no time, or that life is one long slog. The more tired we are, the more tempting this narrative becomes, and I get it. I have spent tedious evenings with a fussy baby who refuses to go to sleep or—even more fun—with three children age four and under who are all refusing to go to sleep. I know people have lengthy and frustrating commutes. Sometimes by the time all the chores are done, we feel like there is limited space before we need to throw ourselves into bed so we can get up and do it all over again.

But the increased time satisfaction in my Evening Hours Challenge suggests a different narrative. No one actually got more time; we all still have 24 hours in a day. People didn't switch jobs. Maybe some compressed chores or got help but there weren't huge lifestyle changes, just as Rebecca wasn't really changing much about her life when she started getting home 15 minutes earlier. The calmer start and 15 minute bonus just prodded her to think about her golden hours in a new way. Once she did, she saw possibilities.

Evenings could become your favorite part of an average workday. But even if they don't, setting a few intentions can help, and alongside these intentions, simply reframing your golden hours as time that should be pleasurable can change the experience of time. Some suffering is unavoidable. But much is not.

This was my takeaway from talking with Faith Hsu, a mother of four school-age children who play a wide variety of sports.

"After doing time logs several times, I realized that I spent a lot of time in the car, sometimes with a child and sometimes by myself," she reports. She sent me a schedule that, sure enough, involved her being in the car from about 2:30 to 7:00 p.m. most weekdays. "On my bad days, I can feel like a resentful taxi driver," she told me, but on her good days, she feels like she gets some me-time or "a wee bit of a date" with a child who's being shuttled or had to tag along. That's something that makes this time feel "useful or valuable rather than a necessity and a chore."

A lot of this comes down to preparation and thinking through pain points—and then realizing that easy tweaks could ease those pain points. For instance, Faith got a second water bottle. In 4.5 hours, "I would get through all of my first and get thirsty." She started bringing snacks that she personally enjoyed, not just those the kids liked. She began packing a sweater. The kids would demand a cranked-up AC after they'd been running around and "I did not want to have the arctic frost on me." She began really curating her audiobook selection, often listening to lighthearted, enjoyable fiction, and—this is key—"I even made a point of knowing where the nice bathrooms are in my journey. Things like not having to use a porta-potty are small but do make a difference." Have a good snack, enjoy a clean and spacious restroom, listen to something funny, and the night isn't so bad, especially if a kid decides to really open up. "That's the pearl," Faith says. "That's my payment for the time I'm in the car—getting those meaningful conversations I might not otherwise get."

How might you, too, insist on a little more pleasure? You might view your commute home as me-time, and listen to a favorite album from your teenage years with lyrics you know by heart. You might read a magazine on the train instead of scrolling through whatever the algorithm dishes up. You might decide to eat dinner outside if the weather is nice, because why not? You might give your preschooler a good long bath on a winter night, featuring a bubble bath scent you actually like, and enjoy relaxing during this time that the child is contained and not getting into other trouble. You can make sure your kids' bookshelves are curated with stories you enjoy, hiding such monstrosities as *The Giving Tree* up on the top shelf. You can open a window as you read in your bed and enjoy the fall breezes. Whenever you find yourself unhappy, or tempted to count minutes until the day is over, you can figure out if there is anything you can do to make the situation better and take those minutes back.

This mindset isn't always easy, but I believe it's worthwhile. Setting intentions "makes the day feel like there's something to look forward to, rather than just a sludge of 'shoulds' to complete the day," one Evening Hours Challenge participant said. "I love my mornings; I used to dread the evenings, but [I] can see how I can bookmark my days with things that are enjoyable. It makes the 'middle' feel more enjoyable as well."

When I asked participants if they thought they could continue with their golden-hour intentions, most agreed that they could, even if tailored to fit their constraints. At the one-month mark, the majority agreed that they were happier with their evenings. People recounted cooking classes, nights devoted to creative projects, and a trip to a baseball game. "Somehow, before this, planning fun for a Tuesday night felt like breaking the rules," one person who joined a trivia league reported. But of course it isn't. There is no rule saying Tuesdays have to be boring or terrible. Rather than being lost, these hours can be golden. Make this little shift and you might be surprised at what is possible.

CHAPTER 6

BE OPEN TO SERENDIPITY

When I take a beach vacation, I like to sit on the beach. I do not like to hurry myself to get ready in the morning. I definitely do not like to ride on small boats out into choppy waters. "Climb into a cage to go swim with sharks" has never been an item on my bucket list.

But my family went to Hawaii for spring break in April 2025, and my oldest, the child who was graduating from high school and would not automatically be with us for any future spring breaks, wanted to swim with sharks. He wisely timed his request to a three-week period when I was making a concerted effort to say yes to more things outside my comfort zone, mostly so I could write about it for my newsletter. I will admit that my reflexive answer would have been that no, I do not wish to swim with sharks. But when I thought about it, I realized I had no reason to say no. I had the time. My son had done his research, and the operator he'd found wasn't too pricey and had hundreds of five-star reviews. It was only a half-day trip, meaning that I would be on the other side of the start-to-finish experience, likely with a margarita, in just a few hours.

And so I agreed—and roused myself early on the Friday morning of our vacation to drive to the North Shore of Oahu from Ko Olina. We checked in, rode the boat about 20 minutes out to a spot where fishing long lines generally drew sharks, and then put on our snorkel equipment. I had to do a lot of encouraging self-talk to get myself to climb into the small cage that was jolting around on the waves as I watched fins circle the boat.

But I did it, and had an experience I will likely remember for years. A dozen-plus Galapagos sharks swam so near the cage that I could look into their eyes and see individual details, like markings on their skin. By the end of our time in the water (during which, yes, I was cold, and got salt water in my eyes, and got stung by some nonshark sea creature), I was starting to recognize some of the more curious sharks as they took laps around. These creatures are magical. So is a day when a 17-year-old is happy to spend time with you. And in the more unexpected category, as we bounced over the waves back to shore, the crew spotted two whales surfacing nearby. Most of Hawaii's humpback whales migrate before late April. And yet there they were, mist blowing from their spouts, tails slapping the water, and their long bodies surfacing again and again. We followed from a respectful distance, all experiencing this awe together.

That's a lot to come out of a little "yes"—a surprisingly delightful adventure and a serendipitous adventure that was just a bonus and never would have happened if I'd stayed on shore. "Yes" makes possible a great many things. Indeed, if you think about it, you'll soon see that almost all new relationships, projects, and shark-swimming adventures come out of a "yes." This is true for personal matters, and in the professional realm as well. Big breaks and big opportunities tend to come from saying yes to something that's not in the normal run of show. After all, if you knew about something already, you'd be doing it. New wins come from being open to what you don't know—in all its messy uncertainty.

This is a topic I keep pondering because, well, I write about productivity. If you read a lot of productivity literature, you know a major theme is that we should all say no more often.

I often press this point in my speeches. People nod as I lament how hard it is to say no, and when I talk about being careful not to overcommit Future You. The usual narrative is that we are all overscheduled and starved for time. A logical solution is to take on less. This leads to reminders that "No is a complete sentence," or advice on how to politely suggest someone else.

Some folks take this tenet of productivity to heart. When I have requested interviews with fellow people in the productivity world, I have occasionally been turned down with lofty statements about how the person is trying to say no to more things in order to make time for what matters. Maybe we all should do the same!

I do get it. I don't want people to spend their precious time on Earth on activities they don't find enjoyable or meaningful. Often, it is wise to say no. Or, as the main character in my time-management fable, *Juliet's School of Possibilities*, put it, "Expectations are infinite. Time is finite. You are always choosing. Choose well."

And yet I see the magic of yes again and again. You agree to a nice-but-not-critical conversation with someone . . . and two years later he's landed at your dream employer and helps you get hired. Or perhaps while finishing dinner at a restaurant, you see a friend's random text asking you to come meet her at a nearby bar. The night has already been long. But you go, and while there you start talking with a gentleman who will, in short order, become your husband and the father of the child who will someday take you out swimming with sharks.

It's hard to see where a given thread will lead, professionally or personally. Life is full of serendipity—roughly defined as finding wonderful things you aren't actively looking for. While the nature of serendipity is that you aren't seeking it, you do have to be open to it. Ideally you practice what I like to call thoughtful accessibility. That means being smart about what you take on, but also making it possible for valuable or agreeable things to reach you.

The good news is that when you develop a mindset of time abundance, secure that you have more than enough time for the basics, you see that you do have space for little wagers that just might lead to something. You can't do everything for everybody. No one can. But in this chapter I'm going to argue that letting random people and opportunities reach you—that is, saying a few more take-a-chance yeses—increases the odds that you can create a schedule you truly love. Sure, you might waste time. But I believe that you have the time, if you choose to see it that way. Across a big time span, being open to serendipity is more productive and probably more enjoyable than walling yourself off in the misguided belief that this is how you get things done.

Getting to a mindset of "yes"

Many years ago, producer Shonda Rhimes famously embarked on a "Year of Yes." Noting that she had a tendency to turn down anything that made her slightly uncomfortable, she hoped to make life more enjoyable by saying yes to random opportunities.

Now, the opportunities that come to Rhimes are probably different from those that come to you and me. But when her book *My Year of Yes* came out, others were inspired to embark on their own "yes quests." For instance, Karen Schneider, a writer for The Muse, did a similar project after starting a new job and feeling a bit lost. She wrote of deciding that "if I had the time and the financial capability to do something, I would just say yes and figure out the details later." She wound up saying yes to networking events, to taking an art class, even to hiking a new trail. Saying yes meant that more opportunities seemed to keep finding her, and life began feeling bigger as a result.

As Schneider discovered, a default mindset of no is a wall. It keeps out bad things, which is helpful. But it will also keep out good things that don't have an explicit invitation. That's a problem, because until you reach the Shonda Rhimes level of fame and power, opportunities tend not to come gift wrapped. Instead, opportunities find you as you talk to new people, follow up, and put some effort in.

I have certainly seen this in my own life. For instance, in October 2018, I got a not terribly promising email from the publicist who'd worked on a book I'd launched that spring. She asked if I wanted to chat with a team from the publishing house's corporate marketing department about "exploring possible opportunities to help you elevate/monetize your podcast *Best of Both Worlds.*"

If I'd been swamped, I might have declined what she said in the email could be "a refresher on stuff you might already know." But I agreed. Soon I was on an email chain with various marketing people who reported that they had evolving relationships with podcast networks. A few calls revealed that they were in talks with a podcast network that was looking to develop a short, daily podcast on successful morning routines—something I had written about before, but which had nothing to do with my existing podcast. I chatted with them and wrote a proposal for a show of productivity tips called *Before Breakfast.* Right around this same time, the network was acquired by iHeartMedia, a much bigger media conglomerate. I recorded some sample episodes for the new owners, and iHeart launched *Before Breakfast* in March 2019. Thanks to iHeart's marketing muscle, we hit number 1 for our category in the first few weeks after launch. Years later, the show continues to be downloaded millions of times annually.

That's great, but was not in any way an obvious outcome of that first email. Or the second. Or the third.

So it goes with many things in life. You don't want to drive yourself crazy with imagining parallel universes. It's impossible to know how any given thing will turn out. If you'd said yes to that party invitation you might have met someone wonderful, but probably not. Perhaps if I hadn't spent my time producing a daily podcast these past few years I would have tried something else that would have made me wildly more successful. Opportunity cost is an uncertain business.

That said, I believe there are a few ways to organize our time so that happy serendipity is more likely to pay a visit. First, we can clear the temporal and mental clutter. Second, we can plan for thoughtful accessibility. And finally, we can develop the mindset of making little bets and observing the outcomes to see what might be worth pursuing more.

1. Clear the clutter

Anyone preaching the virtue of saying no does have this truth on his side: It is hard to make space for randomness when every minute is already spoken for.

The time obligations themselves aren't the biggest problem. You may be leading 18 meetings today, but if you won $100 million in a lottery, contingent on you showing up to collect the prize in person, you'd figure out how to bow out of everything somehow.

But most wins aren't so obvious, and so the problem is more one of mindset. When you feel swamped, you don't read past the second paragraph in that email from a former colleague that's mostly about his recent trip to Cancun, but ends by mentioning that your mutual friend Joe just started working at XYZ company. You definitely don't write an email to Joe to congratulate him on the new gig. You don't agree to meet Joe for coffee next week when he's in town. You're too busy! So you don't talk to Joe, who mentions over coffee that he's just landed a huge contract for something that needs a subcontract in your exact line of work.

When you feel more relaxed about time, though, you don't feel like you need to hoard your minutes. You are more willing to follow these threads to see where they lead.

This means that the first step toward being open to serendipity is to clear the schedule clutter. This is not so much about saying no to new requests—some of which might be cool—as it is about removing things that currently drag on your time. What is making you feel like you can't take on anything new?

If you kept a time log after reading chapter 1, go through it and look for culprits that are sapping your energy or making you feel overwhelmed.

As with gift-wrapped opportunities, I wish clutter was easy to spot. But people's lives are different. If you work in a corporate environment, your decluttering might involve these steps.

Be wary of recurring meetings. Anything that doesn't have to earn a spot on your calendar each time may not deserve a spot on your calendar each time. If it exists it should be short, should involve few people, and should be easily chucked if no one's got a pressing agenda.

Do a little meeting detective work. Why is each meeting happening? Is there an agenda? Are you really needed? If you are working remotely, make sure all those meetings on your calendar actually require every minute assigned to them and aren't quick questions that someone put on your calendar because they didn't want to pick up the phone and call.

Consolidate. Instead of emailing back and forth frequently with people, get in the habit of combining nonurgent matters into one email or one discussion list for a short meetup.

Unplug. Don't check email or instant messages constantly. It makes everything feel more urgent than it is. Even if you need to be fairly accessible, you can check messages for 15 minutes, close out for 45 minutes, then check again.

Block what you can. If you can protect periods of time (e.g., two afternoons a week, or Fridays) from regular time-specific obligations, do it. It is in this open space that you will send the random note that leads to something you wouldn't have imagined.

If you feel guilty about this decluttering, it might help to quantify the opportunity cost of your schedule. Assign any task you have on your calendar a value on a 1- to 10-point scale. Don't value open spaces as 0, against which a 6 looks reasonable. As a smart and ambitious person, you might be able to pursue something in that open space that would wind up being a 9. Is that status meeting with David about a project that is going perfectly fine a 6? If you decided not to do that meeting, then maybe that open space could lead to a 10! Perhaps you could try checking in by email for a few weeks instead and see how it goes.

That said, I know it is not always possible to control one's time at work. Not everyone works in a corporate environment. And in many cases, particularly for those with caregiving or home-management responsibilities, I think it's actually people's *home lives* that make them feel like they can't take on anything new. I was once speaking at a conference for women who were returning to the workforce, and an attendee raised her hand to say that she was nervous because if she went back to work, how were the bathrooms going to get cleaned? While I assured her that her family would figure something out, I do understand this fear of rocking the boat. I tend to feel most unwilling to take on anything new—professionally or personally—at the start and end of the school year, and over the holidays, when there are already many things to juggle. One study from political scientists Anna Helgøy and Ana Catalano Weeks found that the sense of carrying a heavy mental load takes up space in people's minds, and crowds out the desire to take on additional responsibility at work (or participate in public life in general).

If you have a full life, it is not easy to reduce your mental load until it's light enough that you feel open to opportunity. That said, there are a few things you can do.

Don't keep it in your head. Rumination takes up mental space. One reason to create a weekly planning time, as we talked about in chapter 2, is that if you have a regular time for planning life logistics, then you don't need to spend the rest of your time thinking about life logistics. When you find yourself pondering how you'll manage next week's schedule, you can tell yourself there is a time for that, and now is not that time. If stuff occurs to you at some other time? Just jot down a note in your planner or calendar, or email yourself if you are out and about. As long as you have a time when you process your primary inbox, then if you email yourself a task or idea, you will in fact see it.

Batch it. You can also minimize your mental load by batch processing all the little tasks that aren't urgent but do need to get done. I keep what I call a "Friday punch list" with items such as updating my credit card at my web hosting service, signing a kid up for an activity, nicely reminding someone they owe me money, or booking a flight for a future trip. It's more efficient to plow through these things all at once than to do them here and there and feel like you are always doing them. Yes, you have time to follow that random thread because no, you do not need to fill out that permission slip right this second. To make batch processing even easier, keep anything you use frequently (e.g., a picture of your driver's license, your frequent-flyer numbers, or your kids' health forms from the pediatrician) nearby and accessible.

Embrace vertical ownership. If there are multiple adults in your household, each of you can assume complete responsibility for certain spheres, so at least some areas are largely removed from each person's mental load. Maybe one person is completely responsible for all things related to pets. Maybe one person is completely responsible for all things related to groceries.

Don't be cheap. Sometimes you pay more for a comprehensive solution, but the comprehensive solution frees up mental space. Perhaps you continue to pay for a full-time sitter even after your youngest child starts preschool a few mornings a week, because cobbling together part-time options could be complicated and less reliable, and thus require hefty organizational labor on someone's part. If you work for yourself, it might mean hiring an assistant rather than spending lots of time on administrative tasks that other people could do.

Care less. The more you require things to be a certain way, the more things you're going to have to think about. Obviously, some things are hard to get out of, and we do some things even if they are hard, because they matter for closely held values. But when I recently saw another family's elaborate screen-time tracking and rewards system, my first thought was "great for them, not for me." I keep my kids busy, make them surrender their devices at a certain point at night, and let the chips fall where they may. If I don't require people to make their beds daily, then I don't need to spend time tracking whether people have made their beds or not.

The key here is recognizing that mental space is valuable in its own right. Open space invites opportunity in a way that a cluttered mind and a cluttered calendar can't. This is true for professional matters and for personal ones too. You're less likely to strike up a conversation with a person who might become a friend if you're feeling overwhelmed. So be sure you're not cluttering up any sphere of life with more work than necessary.

2. Plan for thoughtful accessibility

Creating open space in your calendar and open space in your mind is the most important thing you can do to welcome serendipity into your life. But much open space will be absorbed by unexpected things that—because of the open space—don't become emergencies. Much of what is left will be used for you to think, or to come up with ideas. Both of these are excellent uses of open space, but not exactly what we're getting at here. So once you've created some space, if you want more serendipitous good things to find you, you can encourage this by structuring your schedule for thoughtful accessibility.

Here's what this means. If someone who didn't know you well had a smart idea, one that you might be able to develop, would they be able to get that idea in front of you? Yes, I know there are many bad ideas in this world. There are also a lot of unpleasant and demanding people. Your time is valuable. This is why people create boundaries. But with all that, is there a possibility you would see it?

Thoughtful accessibility means having boundaries, but not completely walling yourself off. There are a few ways you might do this.

Create specific times on your calendar for "possibility" conversations. If you are in a position of power or authority, and lots of people do want to talk with you, maybe you decide that you will do three 20-minute getting-to-know-you calls per week. That's only one hour, which is not too onerous in the grand scheme of things. You could even decide that unless there's a good reason (I don't like strict rules, as we'll get to later), these calls will happen on Friday mornings. You'd know that Friday morning was "possibility time," and you wouldn't be weighing these calls against all the other things going on in your life. On a slow week, you might even start thinking about who could occupy one of these slots. There are lots of interesting people in the world who might be worth getting to know better.

See email as an opportunity. I know email is one of the world's biggest time sucks. It is also how you are going to communicate with the vast majority of people on this planet who aren't in your immediate circle. Since it is asynchronous, it is a way for people to reach you without too much imposition. Email is how you are going to see that news about a mutual acquaintance that turns out to be important but is buried in an email from someone discussing something else. You should limit how often you check your inbox so email doesn't consume all your time, but you can also develop the mindset that email can bring possibilities, and it might be worth entertaining some of them. If you are managing your own email, you could create an "intriguing" folder and set a time to plow through it. Even if you have an assistant who handles much of your email logistics, don't completely outsource this form of communication. You can handle the back-and-forth with people you know. As for people you don't know, your assistant can flag the random messages that might be interesting or useful. You can then set a time to glance through those and see what you see. Most messages won't lead to anything. But some might.

Move. Serendipity in all its forms is less likely to find you if you are sitting in your office cubicle (or in your home office), productive as these places may be. There is a balance here; the work needs to get done. But you are more likely to be exposed to a random idea or person somewhere else. Sometimes I go work in my local library just for extra stimulation. I might see a new title that prompts me to think of an idea or a potential podcast guest. Or just as frequently, I see a post on a bulletin board that leads to some sort of adventure. One of my children's favorite activities ever was a comic drawing class I saw advertised at the library.

In our digital age, so much is served up based on what an algorithm already knows you want. This is wonderfully efficient, but sometimes it's nice to put yourself in situations that haven't been perfectly tailored to your known desires. You don't know what you don't know. Thoughtful accessibility is the metaphorical equivalent of doing 90 percent of your shopping at Amazon, but then making 10 percent of your purchases at a local boutique or used bookstore. You might not find anything worthwhile, but you might also find something really cool that you never would have thought about. Likewise with a schedule, you spend most of your time on what you know you need to do. But you leave space for what you don't know, and this new stimulus, combined with what you do know, is where the possibilities start to happen.

3. Make little bets

The last step in being open to serendipity is to adopt the mindset that much in life is just little bets. We don't need to expect much from any given thing. It's okay to waste a little time. Most of us waste a lot of time already. Time is big. It is the accumulation of many small bets over the long haul that tips the odds of something wonderful happening in our favor.

One way to get at this low-stakes mindset, versus the scarcity mindset I think a lot of us have, is to consider the situation of a couple who wrote me about a very lucky development: A nearby set of grandparents offered to come over to babysit every Friday night.

Before this development, if the couple wanted to go out for a weekend evening, a date night involved a lot of logistical steps—seeing if there was something they wanted to do, finding a sitter who was available, and then adding the cost of babysitting on to the evening. Because this involved a lot of effort, they had to know the event would be worthwhile to go to all this trouble. So most of the time they didn't bother.

With grandpa and grandma coming over every Friday night from 6:00 to 10:00, though, this couple noted, their decision process changed completely. Is this possibly-great-but-possibly -ho-hum movie worth seeing? Well, the grandparents are coming this Friday, and next Friday, and the next so . . . why not? If the movie turned out to be boring, oh well. They could do something different the next week. With the time already blocked off, the couple began looking for ways to fill the time, rather than making every individual activity justify the price and work of making a plan. As they explained, they could decide to do things like stop by an art exhibit downtown that might be cool but probably wouldn't have justified a date night on its own. While they were out in the world, things would happen—for instance, they might bump into old acquaintances and have a very pleasant conversation that never would have happened if they hadn't done something random.

When it comes to creating luck in life, the sort of luck that makes you fall in love with your schedule, I find it helpful to have the mindset of this couple with the generous grandparents. The metaphorical sitter is booked! You are rich in time. You have more than enough for the basics and then some. I know I do. When I look at my time logs, even after a decade of tracking, I see all kinds of low-value time spent puttering around the house or looking at random influencers. Apparently I am so rich in time that I can read down to the 43rd comment on that *New York Times* article that the algorithm correctly guessed would irk me. Perhaps you have less-than-purposeful hours too.

So, just as a billionaire can take a $50,000 stake in a start-up that sounds interesting without much thought, you too can make little bets with time. You can have a 15-minute conversation with someone without it being an expectation of anything more. You can go to that event that a colleague suggested. You can respond to that unexpected email from someone who enjoys your work. You should be mindful of your safety, but some of my dearest friends are people who've found me through my work, realized they lived nearby or would be in town for something, and reached out to see if I'd be interested in getting together.

Of course the reason people find me is that I have put a lot of content out into the universe. This turns out to be an excellent way to start a conversation, and it's easier for people to do these days than it has ever been before. You can make little bets by writing regular, helpful essays for an industry journal, or as a newsletter. You can pitch yourself to industry podcasts or publications. You don't know who will see what you're putting out there, but probably someone will see it. Indeed, you might be mindful of putting things out to a diverse audience, which can allow for more serendipity than a smaller, closed group. While both are wise to do, a speech to an industry conference just has more legs than the same talk given to a brown-bag lunch for your department. Everyone in your department knows you. Not everyone at the conference does, raising the chances of a new connection.

I realize all these little bets take time, but the mindset of little bets can extend to how we spend time itself. You don't need to write a newsletter for the rest of eternity. Tell yourself you will write weekly for a year and see how it goes. Yes, we will all die at some point, but most of us are going to make it through the next year, and more importantly the year will pass anyway. So if you think it might be fun, go for it. After a year you can quit, pivot, or keep going. You can go on your own "Yes Quest" for a month where you agree to random get-to-know-you meetings, and then you can dial it back the next month as you head into your busy season. You can decide that you'll go to an extra conference this year beyond the usual industry one and just see what comes of it. Most likely nothing, at least not immediately, just as most movies you'd go to because you have the Friday night grandparent coverage won't be great. Angel investors assume 9 out of 10 bets won't lead to much of anything, but the big exit on the 10th company will cover the others. And really, some of those nine other bets won't be worthless. Employee number 4 at a start-up that goes bankrupt will have an idea for another company, she'll call you about investing, and you'll match her up with employee number 5 at another of those bankrupt start-ups. The two of them will give you a solid exit down the road.

So it goes with time. Luck is a long game. It requires recognizing that while some time is simply spent and gone, not all time needs to be spent and gone. When we make little bets, we make small investments that might lead to something. You just don't know what.

A flexible approach to life

Being open to serendipity is, largely, about being flexible with time. Perhaps that sounds odd in a time-management book, as so much of productivity is about deciding what deserves to fill your time and then doing those things when you planned to do them. But if you want to welcome new and exciting things into your life, it's best to be careful about the rules you set. Hold the rules you do set lightly. That's because new and exciting things do not always conform to rules we might set for ourselves.

For instance, I've heard people enamored with a certain conception of work-life balance declare that they do not work past 5:00 p.m. But why? There's nothing magical about 5:00 p.m. Would you turn down a fabulous, career-enhancing project that exactly fits your skills and talents just because you might sometimes work a little later, or perhaps travel on occasion? I think the rational answer is that you'd like to consider it, but if you have spent your career proclaiming that you Do Not Work Past 5:00 p.m. then you might not even be offered the gig.

Lest anyone think that I am only promoting work creep, I can tell you that I have seen these rules go the other way too. Someone might build their life and schedule with the rule that "I can't do anything that's not work during working hours." But if you aren't required to punch in and out . . . why not? Perhaps going to that concert in the church next to your office building in the middle of the day might open up something in your brain that solves the problem vexing you. Perhaps you will meet a new friend or client in the pews. You just don't know.

So be flexible. Keep an open mind. Keep space in your schedule. Try a few yeses. See what happens. You might be surprised.

That was certainly the case for the 200 people I recruited, in early 2025, to go on a Yes Quest with me. For three weeks we would say yes to things that sounded feasible and fun, or at least like they'd make a good story. As I sent encouraging emails recounting my own yeses (such as swimming with those sharks), they sent back tales of their yeses.

One person said yes to breakfast with a friend from graduate school that ended up transforming into a job offer. This person also said yes to a last-minute friend ski trip to California. "I had all the feelings—it would be a little challenging to move schedules around, I was 'abandoning' my family . . . blah, blah, blah. But I said yes and bought the plane tickets." As you might imagine, the trip was a blast.

One person said yes to a difficult conversation that needed to happen and experienced the happy relief of being on the other side.

One person said yes to an evening event at 6:30 p.m. "I didn't want to go back out in the cold after I got home from work but because of the Yes Quest I went. And I am glad I did!"

One person learned that a group helping Haitian refugees learn English was looking for volunteers, "so I inquired and went for the first time today." Saying yes led to such a meaningful experience that "I intend to continue to go on Fridays when I'm not working."

One person went to check out a choir despite never singing before. "It was great!"

One person said yes to taking over the social media accounts of an organization where she volunteered. This turned out to be a huge undertaking, but one that taught her all sorts of new things: "I've improved my photography skills and started to learn new design tools. I find myself frequently brainstorming ideas for posts and stories."

Another person recounted "saying yes to my own ideas," such as inviting people to a local Japanese festival. "For the past three years I have gotten an invitation to the festival and I did not go. Enter the Yes Quest . . . and the five of us who said yes had a great time with the mochi pounding, tea ceremony, sumo demonstration, and a wonderful taiko drum concert."

One of my favorite yeses came from someone who identified herself as the "less fun" parent in her marriage—that is, the one who says no to whatever harebrained schemes other family members dream up. Often someone does have to say no. But occasionally it is good to say yes. This woman recounted that "yesterday, all five of our kids had dentist appointments. The younger four received certificates to go to Raising Cane's for a free kids meal because they had no cavities. The 14-year-old also had no cavities, but since he's considered an adult in the dentistry world, he's too old to get the certificates." Her husband was gone to an overnight conference, so chicken nuggets were on the menu anyway. She figured she might as well say yes to taking the little kids out, even if making an additional evening trip with many small children was going to involve a lot of effort. Since the family had already spent the "eating out" portion of their budget that month, she went home to see if they had any gift cards, and sure enough, she found one for Chick-fil-A, conveniently located a block away from Raising Cane's.

"We got the four younger kids their meals and made our way to the Chick-fil-A drive-through. We ordered and tried to pay with the gift card, but the cashier said it was empty." It turned out that something had gone wrong with transferring the gift-card balance to her online Chick-fil-A account. This could all have been disastrous, but the restaurant workers took one look at the situation and decided that the meal was on the house. "Talk about a real win all around to saying yes in the moment!" she wrote me. "But even more than a free meal, saying yes gave my kids the opportunity to see generosity and goodness in other people. What a gift."

Of course, some things are a definite no. A parent who agreed to volunteer with a child at a local animal shelter did not agree to get a second dog, even though the child made a full PowerPoint presentation with her arguments. Some other folks talked of saying yes to free time after realizing a previously agreed-to obligation was a bad idea. So it goes. No one needs to say yes to everything, or say yes forever. You can simply take a few weeks to be open-minded and see what serendipity finds you.

I do know it is hard to decide what to do when there are many options, and you have a full life. But you might keep this rubric in mind.

In general, you want to spend less time on things you need to talk yourself into. You're not initially excited about a project, but then you start rationalizing that it would look good on your résumé, or that it is the logical next step if you'd like to work abroad someday. The hours are good . . . right? This is how we get a schedule full of things that are a 5 or 6 on a 10-point scale, and don't have space to hunt for or create the 8-, 9-, and 10-point projects that can make a person fall in love with life.

Instead, look for ideas or possibilities that you start talking yourself *out* of. You are immediately excited . . . but then remind yourself how busy you are. Or that you don't think you're qualified, or that you don't think those people will find you interesting, or that it's hard to travel to events when you've got young kids, or you'll have to call in a favor from a coworker . . .

The initial excitement is telling. Everything else is logistics. You'll probably figure it out.

CHAPTER 7

THINK 8,760 HOURS, NOT 24

Angela Justice (as she was then known) spent many years of her career working in the wholesale tea business. She would travel to trade shows and call on countless teahouses, coffee shops, spas, and grocery stores to sell her teas. But as a longtime Buddhist, she was drawn to the monastic life she had learned about. And so, in her late thirties, Angela decided to enter a monastery in the Western United States to begin training. When she turned 39, she was ordained as a novice Buddhist nun, with the new name Jin Zheng Shi, and the goal of becoming a fully ordained bhikshuni.

The daily schedule at her monastery wasn't easy. She would rise around 3:30 a.m. to participate in the morning ceremony (4:00 to 5:00 a.m.). She did her share of the daily ceremonies, communal chores, and the work necessary to host the monastery's retreats. She studied religious matters, learned to lead ceremonies and play the appropriate instruments, and also began to learn Chinese. The final ceremony for the evening would end at 9:30. And then, in whatever pockets of time she could find outside her duties, she needed to do something quite extraordinary.

As part of preparing for ordination, she and the other nuns in her community were required to memorize three whole books of Buddhist teachings on the Vinaya precepts for living a Buddhist monastic life.

This was a lot—about 50,000 words, she told me. In any given moment, on any given day, all this memorization could seem like an overwhelming goal. Indeed, over the years, after finding me through my books and podcasts, Jin Zheng would occasionally write to me about the challenges. "Sometimes I get frustrated because it feels like my progress is so small and incremental," she noted. But, of course, she didn't have to learn this all in one day, and as time kept passing, all these little moments added up. She simply devoted some time to learning the precepts, over and over again, writing down phrases, testing herself on repeating them, and then reciting everything from the beginning. After a year, she had learned a lot. Two years in, she had learned more. At about that point, in late 2022, she learned that she could qualify for ordination in about six months. She undertook a 108-day sprint to finish her memorization. She was ordained as a nun in the summer of 2023.

When I caught up with Jin Zheng in early 2025, I was curious what her life looked like without every bit of her brain being devoted to memorization. Life in the monastery was still intense. In addition to the ceremonies and the chores, the nuns recite the precepts multiple times per month. But Jin Zheng had learned this in the course of her multiyear preparation: Even if any given day feels crunched, in the long run, you can do a lot.

And so she was still fitting in a lot—it was just different things. She had started a master's degree program, taking classes in Chinese and in Buddhist and comparative hermeneutics (featuring such light reading as Heidegger). She sent me a weekly schedule showing time for these classes, and homework, her classical Chinese reading group, her new bhikshuni class for newly ordained nuns, and cantoring a bowing ceremony, among other things.

She was also finding time for personal pursuits that were compatible with monastery life. In 2024 she had managed to read over 300 books. For 2025, she had mapped out how she could use pockets of time to research applying to a PhD or EdD program. She used bits of time to meditate and write "morning pages." She was also thinking of the arc of the year. She developed a plan to work with her writing tutor at the university as she was writing a Buddhist-themed young adult novel (drafting it in the first half of the year, editing it in the latter half). And she was working toward what she called "relationship goals": writing 50 longer, thoughtful emails to extended family members over the course of the year and going on 50 short walks with someone from the monastery or the university.

She had many plans, but if you can memorize three books' worth of precepts, you start to have a sense of how big time can be when you zoom out. After all, 50 long emails, or 50 walks is only one a week of each, with some buffer. Each week, an email or a walk could perhaps be nestled into the schedule between chores and a Chinese class, or after a recitation and before the evening ceremony, or after the evening ceremony if the homework was light.

It couldn't happen every day. But it didn't have to. Over a year there would be time.

"I used to struggle because I thought about everything day by day," Jin Zheng says, and she realized that "I couldn't fit everything into a day." So "I would do the daily stuff. I didn't look long term. I didn't look at the week. I didn't look at the year."

It was a revelation to change this mindset, "to go from day to week and then week to year," she says. She saw what she had done in longer periods of time, and now she could see what she could do. Looking over the next 8,760 hours, "I have so much more opportunity at 45 than I did at 22 just because I know how to plan."

*

I BELIEVE IN THE ABUNDANCE OF TIME, BUT LET ME SAY THIS right now: There are not enough hours in the day to get to everything we want to do. I will also say this: It doesn't matter. Life is not just this one day. While a weeklong time frame (168 hours) is more useful for planning priorities and organizing a schedule, this is not the sum total of life either. Time is much bigger than that.

Most of us are not waking at 3:30 a.m. for morning ceremonies in a Buddhist monastery. But we are often trying to find space to achieve great things professionally, to be a loving and involved family member, to get enough sleep and exercise to stay healthy, to nurture friendships, and to pursue various hobbies. The general narrative is that since time is a zero-sum game, these things are at odds. There will be trade-offs. We will need to pick and choose from this list.

But I believe that a great many stories of time stress come from taking a limited view of time. We look at the moment—or perhaps, the day—that is right in front of us. But while life is never guaranteed, almost all of us will have future moments. Indeed, the odds are good that the vast majority of people reading this book will make it through the 8,760 hours that comprise the next year. We might emerge with some bumps and bruises, but we will most likely see the other side. We can hold two thoughts in mind: that time is finite and precious; but also that in the way we experience life, time is quite vast. A lot can fit in 8,760 hours, and any given 24 hours is far from the full story.

Whenever time feels crunched, or a trade-off feels challenging, or you are feeling overwhelmed, try zooming out. Look at time more broadly. I'm not saying you'll read 300 books a year while becoming fluent in Chinese. But there is a very good chance that life will start to feel full of possibility.

A lot of not-last days

Our culture has all sorts of morality tales warning those who might assume anything about the future. Consider that gem about the gentleman who finds a newspaper from today's date a year from now. He eagerly starts making trades based on future stock prices . . . until he turns to the obituary section and reads his own.

It is true that no one knows the future. Tomorrow is never promised, a truth that feels more urgent every time disasters hit the headlines. You read that 60-plus people, much like you, got on a plane and then died in a crash. Or there are the more common tragedies that never make the news. A cousin is diagnosed with an aggressive form of cancer and is gone in a few months. We hug our kids a little tighter. We ponder how sad it would be if someone had always wanted to write a novel, or visit New Zealand, and, busy with the busyness of life, never did.

So, should we "live each day as if it were our last?" A moment's thought reveals that this widely attributed motivational quote, which seems like a logical conclusion from the truth that tomorrow is not guaranteed, is completely unworkable. I want to visit New Zealand, but I wouldn't want to spend my last day on earth on an airplane.

In any case, I prefer the mindset of a cartoon I came across on Instagram featuring bootleg Peanuts characters. Charlie Brown says "Some day, we will all die, Snoopy!" The dog replies "True, but on all the other days, we will not."

Most likely, there will be a lot of not-last days. The Social

Security Administration publishes actuarial tables showing your probability of dying in the next year. With the figures used in the 2024 Trustees Report, a 46-year-old woman's odds of making it through the year are well over 99 percent (her actual death odds are 0.002994, if you'd like to be exact). The odds change as you get older, of course. The average life expectancy in the US is about 78 years—roughly the 4000 weeks that Oliver Burkeman made famous—but once you have made it to any given age, which, since you are reading this, seems to be the case, your odds of making it to your *next* birthday tend to be good. A 65-year-old man's death odds in the next year are 0.019914 (about 2 percent). Even an 85-year-old woman has a 92 percent chance of making it to 86. The Katy Perry lyric "All we have is this moment" is just, statistically speaking, unlikely. An actuary once told me that anyone saying "All we have is this moment" probably wants to buy something expensive.

Which could be fun! I'm not here to judge. I also know that there are life-altering events (good and bad) that can shape the next year even if one lives through it. A new job, an unexpected pregnancy, or a serious illness will all change the daily experience of time. But given that we are highly likely to make it through the next year, even with the unknowns, we can start thinking through the next year with a rational sense of what it will look like. From studying people's time, and their goals, I've also come to see that a year is about the length of time that people can plan with reasonable clarity. It's hard to see well beyond that, but you can picture 8,760 hours. Most likely the next year will feature a lot of the same ground rules that you're living with now. Most likely if you're going to do something big, it will be on your horizon with about a 12-month lead time.

There are also some real upsides to viewing time in terms of 8,760 hours. Any given day can be taken in context. Even a busy season can be taken in context. We start to see how much time there is and, more excitingly, can start to ask what we want to do with it.

The view from a high-rise window

Because I have tracked my time for a decade, I've gotten a sense of what thinking in terms of 8,760 hours actually means. When you are in any given day, marching through the day's calendar, it's like shouldering your way down a busy sidewalk at rush hour. The 8,760-hours perspective is being up on the 30th floor of a high-rise. You see the whole and varied neighborhood, with its crowded spots, more open parks, bigger buildings, smaller storefronts, and perhaps some trash-filled alleys, depending on where we're going with this metaphor.

To help me view my time from this perspective, I recently tallied up how I spent the 8,784 hours of 2024 (it was a leap year; hence the extra 24 hours).

As we talked about in the first chapter on changing the narrative, many stories I could tell myself did not survive an encounter with data. I feel like I spend a lot of time working. On a "normal" workday I aim to work at least 8 hours. I often work on weekends—logging at least some work on 34 of the 52 Saturdays of 2024. And yet with all this, 2024 featured a lot of "abnormal" workdays when I worked less. I logged 1,525.5 hours during the course of those 8,784 hours, which (subtracting some vacation days) comes out to about 32 hours a week.

Sleep was all over the place from a daily perspective. On the handful of days featuring overnight flights or a sick preschooler (or my own sick self), I logged fewer than 4 hours of sleep. On a catch-up day I once logged 11.75 hours. The weekly tallies ranged from 46.5 hours to 56.5 hours, but curiously enough, this averages out to 51.38 hours per week, or 7.33 hours per day, which is almost the exact same amount I clocked in 2016, 2017, 2018. . . . My set point is what it is over any longer stretch of time. In total, I slept 2,683.5 hours in 2024.

Subtracting 1,525.5 and 2,683.5 from 8,784, you get 4,575 waking, nonworking hours. I spent what felt like a lot of that driving around in the car, or trying to get my preschooler to go to sleep at night, but with all that, 4,500-plus hours still leaves a lot of time for other things. I spent about 80 hours running—the most in the weeks leading up to an October half-marathon, and the least (zero) in the two months I took off due to debilitating back and nerve pain. I logged 125.25 hours at choir practices or practicing choir music on my own. I spent 128.25 hours doing puzzles. I spent a full 1.5 of those 8,784 hours in line for the Haunted Mansion at Disney's Magic Kingdom, though not on purpose.

Perusing the logs definitely brought up memories. It was a year of adventures, from seeing the northern lights in Maine to riding in a horse-drawn carriage through Seville. It was also a year of a lot of "scroll/relax" as I sometimes put it. I am not proud of the volume of time spent following each day's outrage on X, but seeing the full 8,784 hours made me more accepting of this. I wasted a lot of time in 2024, and I did a lot, because 8,784 hours is a lot of time. I spent gobs of time on pointless things *and* it was one of the most productive years of my life. Many things that seem contradictory are in fact perfectly compatible when viewed from a broader perspective.

I see this all the time with matters of work-life balance. When I was first writing about this topic, I got to talking with a woman who was newly promoted to management and had recently had her first child. She knew that her team members wanted her to take them out to dinner to acknowledge their hard work, and she knew it would be good for her to spend relaxed time with her team. That way, when she had to give tough feedback, they'd know it came from a good place. But she was already working full time, and if she took her team out to dinner, she wouldn't be home putting her baby to bed. That would make her a bad mother! But if she wasn't taking her team out, she was a bad boss! This sounded like one of those anecdotes that start essays about how no one can have it all. She had talked herself into quite a corner, but after listening for a while, I wondered: Did her team want her to take them out *every single night*? As in 7 nights a week, 30 a month, and 365 a year? That seemed unlikely. If she took her team out once every two weeks or so, that meant she was still home putting her baby to bed 13 out of 14 nights. To me, that sounded like almost all the time. Looking at the one moment when things were in conflict limited her life. Zooming out made it possible to see that she could be both the boss and mom she wanted to be.

Or consider Torrey Boland Birch, an academic neurointensivist who shared her schedule with me. Her ICU service schedule involves doing seven straight days of clinical work, which includes being on call 24/7, with emergency calls overnight and long days in the ICU. Perhaps this seems like a challenging job to have, given that she also has three young children, one of whom has special needs. Working seven days in a row might not be sustainable over the long term. But her clinical service contract isn't for every week, all 52 weeks of the year. She does 15 weeks a year, which is 105 days. The other 37 weeks of the year she focuses more on the administrative aspects of her job as director of the ICU and is able to work more on her own schedule (or is off), which means that for 260 days a year she is not in the hospital all the time and has a lot of control of what she does. "This has freed me up to be able to get to all of my children's medical and therapy appointments," she reports, "and to be present in their lives." Zooming out to see the whole year means she can use her skills to treat desperately sick or injured people, earn a good living, and be the mom who's there at the 3:00 p.m. Tuesday speech-therapy session—and understand that none of these goals are in conflict.

Zoom out

I am not saying you have to track 8,760 hours, or even longer, to gain this perspective, though you could. Once I began tracking time continuously, I realized that I had inadvertently joined a community of people who really want to know where the time goes. As you might imagine, some members of this community are on the eccentric side. Consider Aleksandr Lyubishchev (1890–1972), a Soviet scientist who tracked 56 of his 82 years on this planet. A breathless string of posts on Threads claims he "developed a productivity system like no other" and that his time tracking and time management "made him one of the most efficient scientists in history," but . . . you probably haven't heard of him. However efficient he was, his Wikipedia page notes that "his main work remained unpublished."

I suppose I have my eccentricities too. But I promise that many normal people have tracked their time for at least a year and have developed a new perspective as a result of this zooming out.

Nina Khashchina read *This Strange Life*, Daniil Granin's book about Lyubishchev (which plays up his "mad scientist" image) and decided she also wanted to track her time. The goal was to make space for her varied interests: running, blogging, and volunteering, alongside work and parenting. She used an app called *Timelogger*, and kept "a close-to religious record" of her activities for about two years. An artist, Nina found that before time tracking, her time felt like a broken stained-glass window, and she had no sense of the actual picture. "But time tracking helped me to see that the picture is actually visible," she told me. Even if one corner looks like nothing, when she zoomed out, "a larger view shows that it is a part of this or that and it actually moves me in the right direction—to a picture I want to build."

Nina had been tracking in five-minute intervals, but eventually found this unsustainable. She switched to broad brushstrokes for a while, then returned to time tracking with thirty-minute intervals at the end of 2021. The timing was fortuitous. Nina is Ukrainian American, and most of her family was still in Ukraine at that point. The beginning of the war in early 2022 "changed our lives completely," but after the initial chaos, she was able to use her logs to monitor some of the manifestations of her anxiety that weren't helping anyone. "For example, I saw that I started following air raids on a city where I grew up and did not stop even after my parents were evacuated. I did not know that I was doing it until I saw it in my log as a separate item." She knew that she didn't have time for this, especially as she became a caregiver for three older non-English-speaking adults who joined her in the US. She remains vigilant, studying the data to see if something is a regular peak and trough, or something requiring action. When she noticed that breakfast was suddenly taking a lot longer, she realized that she was reading all sorts of news sources, so she decided to limit herself to one major and one local news source. "Breakfast time is back to what it was," she reports.

Christen Kisch, an English teacher, medical translator, and medical student in Italy, has tracked her time since October 2019 (minus about six weeks total, including a month in 2022 when her first son was born). "I originally started tracking my time to see where on earth it was all going, because I remember somehow feeling very harried even pre-children and pre-having a serious partner." She notes that "this seems laughable, looking back, now that a toddler takes up so much of my brain," but "once I started, I really enjoyed having that information collected there in case I ever wanted to look at it again, so I just kept going."

There have been obvious shifts as life changed over the years. She used to volunteer for many hours with the Italian Red Cross's ambulance service, something she has put on hold for a few years in order to spend more time with her growing family. But other things were remarkably constant. Minus a few weeks of infancy, she found that with a baby "your sleep kind of does settle into whatever your sleep is going to be," even if it's disjointed, a pattern that she found "comforting." During the first year of her son's life, Christen said, "I tended to get roughly in the same range of sleep as ever. So there's no need to panic over it. If there's one bad night, I'll feel a little crummy the next day but life will go on."

Looking over longer periods of time has also helped her feel more peaceful about time spent with extended family. Christen's parents live in New Jersey. "They're not going to be with us forever," she notes, and so moving to Italy to be with her husband a few years ago was a big decision. "But since tracking my time I've noticed that, yes, there are months when our only contact is a few video calls each week, but when I go back and visit them, we're together 24/7 minus sleep, and that concentrated time together is all the more precious to us." She spent three weeks visiting her parents over Christmas. "How many adult children get to spend three solid weeks with their parents?" Even people who live 20 miles away might not hit as many hours over a year as she clocks in two or three longer visits (including when they come see her). Zooming out helps her see that.

Zooming out can also show that even bits of time accumulate. Sten Bolander works in IT for a health-care company. He also has a second job as a church musician, which involves playing the organ, accompanying the choir, and choosing hymns. He relies on time tracking to make sure that all his varied work tasks take the amount of time he thinks they should and that nothing is getting too out of control. He's found that long-term tracking has reduced his urge to multitask: "When I'm tracking, I'm doing less changing from one thing to another, because I don't want to have to write that down," he says. He tells himself, "Let's not get sidetracked to doing something else until whatever you're working on is done." But even if something is just fit in for five minutes here and there, over the long term, that isn't nothing.

Sten uses the time-tracking app *ATracker*, which allows for very detailed reports on any category he's created. He created a category called "genealogy" to track time spent updating and analyzing the family tree. It wasn't a category he was emphasizing in his current schedule, but when we talked, he was able to run a report of time spent on genealogy from March 2024 to March 2025. By zooming out, he found that the answer was four hours and seven minutes, or about an hour a quarter. "If you're not looking at things, if you're not aware, you don't think you're doing anything, but a little bit of time here, a little bit of time there, adds up."

Make rational plans

When you know what life has looked like over a longer stretch of time, then you can start to look forward in longer stretches and think about what you'd like to see. That is, since I have a reasonable sense of how I spent the last 8,760 hours and what can fit in 8,760 hours, I can make rational allocations of how I will spend the next 8,760 hours. The far future is hard to see clearly as the variables stack up, but we can see a year with enough clarity that we can start to ask what we'd like a year to look like. Many people do this at obvious fresh-start times, such as on January 1, or at the start of an organization's fiscal year. But you can use any moment to think about the next 8,760 hours. What would you like the next 8,760 hours to look like?

Even if you aren't reading this book on January 1, I encourage you to spend some time thinking about this question, and about what you'd like to see happen both professionally and personally. A few exercises can help.

On the professional front, you might picture yourself 8,760 hours into the future, thinking back and saying, "Wow, that was a really good year!" In terms of how you spent your time, what made the year so amazing? Perhaps you are marching into your supervisor's office to ask for a promotion and a raise. You know she will say yes because you did X, Y, and Z. What are those things? Or maybe you've kept things as they are at your current job, or you've scaled back modestly, and you've devoted significant time to a side project you're passionate about. What could you have accomplished over a year?

On the personal front, you might picture yourself getting together with an old friend on this day a year in the future. As you're chatting about life, he says he's never seen you look so happy. What's your secret? You talk about the amazing things you did over the past 8,760 hours: the weekly dates you and your spouse have gone on, how you're playing in a community volleyball league with your teenage daughter, or how you have fully embraced your hobby as an amateur magician and you've been pulling rabbits out of hats at fairs all summer (to each their own!).

Make a list of whatever would have you feeling celebratory. Then think about how much time these things would take. How much time would you need to clock to make them happen? Some things are uncertain, but you might be able to estimate. And often these estimations, even if they feel big as you experience them, will seem quite reasonable in the context of 8,760 hours.

For instance, based on a friend's experience, perhaps you decide to devote 5 hours a week for 20 weeks to job searching and see what happens. In the middle of those hours, this might feel long and frustrating (a topic we'll return to in the next chapter). Time as we are experiencing it can feel vast. Just picture yourself logging an hour sending in résumés after a full day of work, when you have done this for the past 87 work days. In the moment it might feel eternal, but 100 of 8,760 hours is only 1.14 percent of your total time. If you sleep 8 hours a night, it's only 1.71 percent of your waking 5,840 hours, and in those 100 hours (and hopefully less), you might find something that makes you excited to get out of bed.

Or consider people who write novels for National Novel Writing Month. They often spend two to three hours per day writing during the 30 days of November. This means a rough novel draft might be doable in 90 hours. Give yourself 200 hours and you might produce something more readable. I can tell you that if you sit down to write a draft and set a timer for two hours, it is going to feel like an eternity until that buzzer goes off. And yet you could do this, day after day for 100 days, and still have thousands of waking, nonworking hours left over.

My 80 hours of running in 2024 (and another 50 or so of strength training) meant I could run a half-marathon, albeit slowly. Aim for 4 to 6 hours of running a week and you could probably run a full marathon. I looked through the "advanced" training plan for a 50-mile race that Joel Thomas from chapter 1 sent me and found it maxed out at 13 to 14 hours a week over a 20-week training cycle. When you're 2.5 hours into a 4-hour run, that run could feel endless, but in the context of an 8,760 hour year, it's not much at all.

If you want to go back to school, you could figure out how much time each class and the associated coursework would take. Even something like 18 hours a week for 36 weeks of the year comes out to 648 hours. I'm not saying it would be easy to make that fit. It won't be easy. But if a year has 8,760 hours, sleeping 2,920 (8 hours per night) and working 40 hours for 49 weeks

(1,960) leaves 3,880 hours. You could spend 28 hours per week with family (1,456 hours) and then hunt for those 648 hours among the remaining 2,424. During the semester's busy weeks something else might get fewer hours, be that work, sleep, or family. But during other weeks, those things will get more time, and the year will happily fit it all.

Now, to be clear, no one has to do any of this. Perhaps those previous paragraphs made you excited, and you are on the website for your local community college right now. But I'm guessing that some people don't want to cram more into their lives.

So before you throw this book across the room, I want to emphasize that there are reasons beyond fitting more in to start looking at life more broadly. Zooming out makes trade-offs in general feel less harsh, whatever those trade-offs happen to be. People talk themselves into believing in the existence of all sorts of these trade-offs. If I work full time I'll never see my family. If I am trying to grow a business, I won't have time for friends, or to take care of my health. If I move to Italy, I'll be abandoning my family in the United States.

But when you zoom out, the trade-offs that appear stark in any given moment start to become more nuanced. I know many accountants spend the months of January to March or April questioning their life choices. But when you look at the year as a whole, you can acknowledge a busy season there, and perhaps in the fall, and then savor the weeks in summer that are much slower. A lawyer who bills 300 hours a month while on location for a trial might decide to feel perfectly fine billing 100 hours the next month and still be on track for the year's billable target. That rough month and the quieter month are all part of the same 8,760 hours, and looking at 8,760 hours gives a more accurate perspective than drawing conclusions about life by looking at one month or the other.

A happy sense of possibility

When we decide to view time more broadly than the present moment, we do need to have certain beliefs about the near future. We have to believe that it will exist and that we, with bodies and brains similar to our current ones, will be living in it in similar ways to how we do now.

This seems obvious, but a lot of time-management disasters actually stem from people *not* believing this. They believe their future selves will be entirely different people, with more time and energy, and perhaps access to more than 24 hours in a day. It takes a certain amount of discipline to decide that one won't magically be able to memorize three books of precepts in a few days in the future, so if you'd like to see it happen, best to do some today, and some tomorrow, and so on for three years. You will feel exactly the same about it in 18 months as you do right now, so you figure out what you can do right now, and you just keep doing that.

But when you know where your time goes, I believe you can start to make rational bets about the future. You can decide that a time crunch today is not all there is, and given that you have evidence that there have been less crunched moments in your recent past, it's likely that there will be another less crunched moment in the future. You can look to the future to feel sanguine about the present.

I know not all time trackers feel that way. There's a quote attributed to our mad scientist friend Aleksandr Lyubishchev that says, "He who reconciles with reality does not believe in the future." On some philosophical level, yes—we are always deciding what to do in the present moment and then moving on to the next present moment. But if future time is a construct, it's a pretty useful one. The future is unknowable, but if I don't believe in the future enough to sign my kids up for summer camp, then when time passes and summer does happen, as it often does, I won't be able to write any deep thoughts about the nonexistence of the future, as I will have a crowd of people underfoot asking me to drive them to Starbucks or open their packages of Goldfish.

As it is, we can believe two truths: The future is uncertain but we always live in probabilities. No one knows the future but long-term time tracking has shown me what the contours of my future will most likely look like. If I have slept 7.3 to 7.4 hours per day on average for the past decade, most likely I will sleep for 2,664.5 to 2,701 of the next 8,760 hours, meaning I have 6,059 to 6,095.5 waking hours to play with.

So what will I do with them? What will you do with your next 8,760 hours? When we look forward and see how vast this time is from the perspective of how we live our days, we start to feel a happy sense of possibility. The time crunches and hard trade-offs are often illusions. Any given moment, or any 24 hours, is not all we have. Time is a lot bigger than that.

CHAPTER 8

BE PATIENT

Eastern box turtles do not hibernate. They "brumate." This is a period of winter dormancy during which their metabolism slows, though they are not actually asleep. They burrow into soft soil, mud, or leaf piles, and just generally relax there, conserving energy until spring.

I learned of brumation while interviewing essayist Mary Laura Philpott for my *Before Breakfast* podcast. Mary Laura lives in Nashville, Tennessee, where there are a lot of eastern box turtles, and in particular a more gregarious turtle named Frank ("I'm sure not what his turtle Mama named him, but we had to call him something"), who has adopted the Philpott family. Frank sports a rather distinctive shell pattern, which is how they know it is him. He meanders around the patio during warmer months. Then he disappears sometime in autumn. They wait, wondering. One never knows what will befall a turtle in the cold, or under the wheel of a car. But so far, Frank has brumated and then, like spring daffodils, come back.

When we talked, Mary Laura allowed that she, too, was brumating, at least metaphorically. Her previous books, *I Miss You*

When You Blink and *Bomb Shelter*, had scored effusively positive reviews. The exact quote about *Bomb Shelter* in *The Washington Post* was that it was "a precious gift to the world." NPR named it one of the best books of the year.

But . . . then it was time to write the next thing. Mary Laura had not written the next thing. As a fan who was hoping to read the next thing, and as a writer haunted by a professor's advice that "your last piece will never write your next one," I wondered how she was feeling about all this.

The surprising answer was that she seemed to be feeling okay. In early 2025, she posted on Instagram that she'd had a "nice, gentle year creatively." She had started a few things percolating, but "I don't feel any sense of urgency about it—no hustle-hustle-hustle—just curiosity." This caption accompanied photos of her looking very relaxed.

When I interviewed her, she reported that it had indeed taken some work to get to this place of peace. For a while after her last book came out, when she was not cranking away at a new one, she felt like "ooh, I am breaking a rule! I didn't email my agent today. I'm going to get in trouble!" But then she realized she was not going to get in trouble "because there's actually no one watching and monitoring and going 'how much time did you log at your computer today?'" As time kept passing, she decided that "I don't have to rush it." Instead, she could ask, "What would my brain do if I let it just wander around, and if I let it consider concepts and even future projects without any sense that they might actually happen or succeed?"

And so, for about a year and a half at that point, that is what she had done. Most days she would go for a long walk with her dogs, read, and then sit at her computer playing around with ideas. She would see what would happen with zero expectations. Then she'd have dinner with her husband, go to bed, and get up and do it again.

Through this time of brumation—this period of creative dormancy—she was holding two thoughts in mind simultaneously.

First, she was not done. She had not retired. "I've lived enough cycles of life and creativity and lessons learned to trust that I'll just know, the same way I knew it was time to pull back. There will be something that makes me go 'Oh, I want to call my agent today.'" She knew for certain that there would be a next thing, and it would be as "genius" (to quote *The New York Times*) as her other creations. Somewhere out in the future, written in her book of hours, there would be another Mary Laura Philpott project that could stand next to her previous ones.

She also had no idea what the timeline would be. It could happen tomorrow. It could happen in a year. Until then, she could simply have faith that it would happen. And so, with that established, she could be gentle, creatively. "I'm in turtle mode," she told me. "I'm in slow mode. I'm inside my shell." She could be curious about the ideas that came to her, knowing that, like Frank, she would emerge when the weather was favorable. "I'm not a patient person," she told me. Neither Frank nor the rest of us has eternity, at least on this earth, but Mary Laura noted in her Instagram post that "there's plenty of time. Nothing's as complicated as you think it is."

Active patience

Patience may be a virtue, but like Mary Laura, I would not call it my favorite virtue. Thrift or diligence? I am all in. But in general, if I want something to happen, I would like it to happen right now. Yesterday would have been better. Since you are reading a productivity book, I am guessing you feel the same.

For many things in life, it *is* good to do them right away. Swift transitions make a complex life possible.

However, there are also things that simply take as long as they take. They frustrate our attempts to impose a timeline. How long will it take to meet someone special? To find a job you are excited about? To come up with a career-making breakthrough? To recover from an illness where the diagnosis itself isn't even certain? For a preschooler to stop being afraid of monsters living in the closet? I have no idea. No one does.

But when we realize that time is big and abundant, then we can afford to be generous with it. That can mean being helpful (people are a good use of time!), or following a thread to see where it leads. It can also mean being patient with others, with ourselves, and with how long things take. Indeed, a good working definition for patience is being generous with time. One can feel certain of the outcome, and yet know that outcome might not happen tomorrow. Or in a week. Or in a month. In the course of a year, though, a lot can change with effort. In longer stretches of time, the odds continue to increase.

I call this *active* patience. You can have faith in the outcome, and take steady steps toward your goal, but still hold the timeline lightly, understanding that life is often about probabilities.

Patience is challenging. As a time-management strategy, it's harder than tracking your time or instituting a weekly planning session. There is also a fine line between patience and procrastination. Patience isn't staring at a blank page and quitting three minutes later to go organize your spice drawer. It isn't flitting between applications 1,200 times a day when the answers don't come quickly. It also isn't about imagining that life will manifest whatever you want without you lifting a finger. It's about trying things out, and sticking with them, and putting in the effort. But with that, we can recognize that the first iteration of whatever we crank out might not be great. The second might also be lacking. This can continue for a while.

So what? If you can keep trying and persist at something you think is worth persisting at, you will find that patience is a super-power in a world where many people quit or get distracted. It is a superpower accessible to anyone who believes he or she has all the time in the world, or at least as much as anyone else. There is much happiness to be gained from realizing that for many types of success, time is the secret ingredient. You do what you can do, and then you let time work its magic.

Time is good at its job

When it comes to the topic of patience, Frank and his brethren are excellent role models. People associate turtles with moving slowly, which is not always true, but many turtle species are play-ing on a different timeline than we are. A sea turtle or large land tortoise's lifespan might be 150 years. According to Guinness World Records, a Seychelles giant tortoise named Jonathan was, in 2025, the oldest verified living turtle, plodding on north of his 190th birthday, but some other turtles may have lived longer than that. We just don't know. Records of human births from 200 years ago can be patchy, let alone turtle births. Turtles can heal from serious injuries. It just takes time, which, fortunately, turtles have in abundance. Day by day, time works its magic, a cracked shell heals, and a turtle lives for another five decades.

So it goes for many things. Nature is full of examples of active patience—like seeds that with daily doses of water and sun grow to become towering trees over decades. No one berates a tree for not growing overnight. It takes time, but give a sapling time and magic will happen. We can recognize that time can work its magic with all sorts of other things in life too, even if the process isn't quite as linear as the growing height and girth of a tree. For instance, in one study, researchers looked at what happened to people who rated their marriages as "unhappy" over the course of five years. As you might imagine, some of these couples got divorced. But of those that didn't get divorced, five years later two thirds of these people rated their marriages as "happy." This obviously wouldn't be the case for abusive situations, but these run-of-the-mill unhappy marriages had simply been at a low point. Perhaps other things changed too, but alongside those changes time worked its magic to pull things out of a slump.

When I wrote about this finding in a newsletter, a woman wrote back that she had seen something similar in her life. "At this time five years ago my husband was sleeping in the basement; he did so for [about] eight months," she told me. "Thanks to patience and time (and learning new skills and no one doing anything foolish like having an affair) we got through it, reconciled, and are in a good place as we face a soon-to-be empty nest. I am sure a divorce would have been horribly disruptive, and think a main factor was my husband being unhappy in his work and that spilling out to unhappiness with the marriage. One of the things that helped me get through was friends sharing stories of their parents or siblings also going through rough patches (one friend's parents were separated for nine years!) and ultimately reconciling."

Like a cracked shell, a broken marriage doesn't heal overnight. But it might eventually.

Patience isn't passive

Of course, it is one thing to praise patience looking back on a tough time from a better place. I tend not to get notes from people saying, "Hey, my spouse and I are screaming at each other every night right now. But I'm sure in five years we'll be reconciled!" That said, I do think there are ways to tap into this superpower long before a happy outcome has happened.

First, we can recognize the "active" part of active patience. This isn't a passive process. We need to do our jobs so time can do its job too. I think about the experience of a woman who wrote to me about taking a high-stakes professional exam three times. When she first took it in 2022, she failed it by three points. Then she took it again six months later and failed it by one point. "I was so defeated and took a break from it completely and after some vacation and reflection I decided to try it again," she reports. "I revised my study plan in January 2024 by finding a prep course and a study skills course." On the third try, two years after the first try, she passed. She noted that "with time I became less intimidated by the test and became more confident with the material." But while it is true that time and experience helped, she did plenty too. She and time made a team.

We can imagine how this plays out in many spheres. Indeed, if you're going through a tough time and trying to adopt this spirit of active patience, it might help to keep this "team" imagery in mind. You and time are playing as a doubles tennis team against whatever challenge you're facing down. Or perhaps if you prefer a more martial metaphor, you and time are buddies in a foxhole, doing battle against your problems together. *This* is active patience.

For instance, if you would like to meet someone special, active patience means believing that someday you will. You can see yourself dancing at your wedding. In the meantime, you are systematic about going on enough first dates that you find a reasonable number of people you want to go on second dates with. You go on enough second dates until you find people you want to go on third and fourth dates with. You don't get discouraged at devoting three to four hours a week to random coffee dates, because it's all part of the process. You're doing your work so time can do its work too.

Or maybe you have been laid off and need a new job. Active patience means trusting that eventually, in the not-too-distant future, you will be working somewhere amazing. You will be doing interesting projects with clever colleagues and being paid well for your efforts. In the meantime, you commit yourself to a few hours each day of job searching and informational interviews and sending in résumés. You do the work, and then you can relax and enjoy going to the gym, or volunteering in your kid's class during the extra time you have available, knowing that time will be putting in its hours too.

When we adopt this mindset of active patience, with time beside us in the foxhole, we can even be philosophical about set-backs. No one wants to watch a movie where the hero succeeds at the beginning and then keeps succeeding straight to the end. Obstacles improve the plot. Active patience means envisioning that your story will follow the same format as any hero's journey. In the movie's later scenes, you will be laughing with Mr. or Ms. Right about that hilariously bad blind date on Valentine's Day. Your future colleagues will be hanging on that tale of the interviewer who rescheduled six times. Isn't it lucky the first time didn't work? Because that's when you wound up chatting with a former manager who mentioned that her neighbor worked for this cool new start-up and . . . the rest is history.

Tapping into patience as a superpower means realizing that you can tell yourself such stories *even while you are in the middle of them*. You don't need to punish yourself for the fact that the process is taking awhile. You are doing your part and time is doing its part, and you are just in the middle of the plot. Even during that bad blind date, as you are figuring out how to extricate your-self from the restaurant, you can be telling this story from the perspective of Future You. Indeed, you might actually try writing this story. When a setback happens, shape it into an anecdote. Sit down and write an email to yourself with the details. Show how this narrative moment is leading, inexorably, toward the happy conclusion. When you are patient—certain of the outcome, but calm about the timeline—all of this is just material. The more ludicrous it is, the better the story. Indeed, there is some research finding that anticipation accounts for the bulk of the happiness derived from good events (such as planned vacations). So if you can convince yourself that the outcome is certain, the stretch of wondering beforehand can be recast as time spent anticipating future pleasure. It's kind of like knowing you have a great vacation booked in a few months.

I am not saying this is easy. So it might help to turn active patience into something of a game. (Fun fact: "Patience" is actually the European name for the card game that North Americans call "Solitaire.") You can keep a list of the steps you are taking toward the future outcome. You can give yourself Patience Points for doing a certain number of things per week: two first dates, perhaps, or two informational interviews, or five one-hour sessions at your laptop writing. Then you can give time points for doing its job too. Each day that you have stuck with it, avoiding despair, your teammate earns another Patience Point. You can celebrate at regular intervals. At 20 points you go visit a friend who lives an hour away. At 50 you go to a movie you've been wanting to see. You keep celebrating until the makeshift celebrations aren't necessary, because you are celebrating the thing you were trying to achieve.

Time is on our side

On Saturday, January 13, 2024, I woke up with a strange and sharp pain down my right leg. I'd been dealing with back pain for much of the previous year. It was often bad enough at night that I'd be leaning obviously to one side. But this was new. I limped through the morning's activities, and by afternoon the pain had subsided enough that my time log shows I made it downtown to the Philadelphia Auto Show. Then, that night, as I tried to give the little kids a bath and they were misbehaving, and I kept bending over the side of the tub to intervene, something gave out. The nerves on my leg started firing. I could not even make it down the stairs. Somehow, I got my youngest into bed, then collapsed into my own bed, where I spent the night biting back screams as each attempt to find a comfortable position resulted in new waves of excruciating pain.

The next week was rough, and I say this as someone who's experienced natural childbirth. I could not shower. I could barely make it to the bathroom without screaming. Eventually, my husband helped me limp into a physical medicine specialist's office, and he prescribed the usual mix of steroids, painkillers, X-rays, physical therapy, etc.

Over the next few days, the steroids calmed the initial inflammation (likely swelling pressing on a nerve). The pain stopped feeling like a white-hot poker and more like a constant, dull companion—but I do mean constant. Basically, doing anything hurt.

So, over the course of the spring, after months of physical therapy didn't help, and after X-rays and an MRI didn't pinpoint an obvious cause, I decided that I needed to reach some level of acceptance with my chronic pain. I could hold two thoughts in mind simultaneously—my version of active patience.

One was to believe that I could get better eventually. People do. As a generally healthy person, my odds were as good as anyone else's. I could envision some future time when I would be frolicking around, pain-free, and I could work toward that goal by continuing to be as active as my body would allow.

The second was realizing that, in the meantime, it was quite possible that I was going to have to live for a long and uncertain amount of time with pain that made bending over to empty the dishwasher problematic. Since I didn't want to stop living my life (even if I would have been happy to stop emptying the dishwasher), I would have to learn to just do what I could with pain as my backdrop. When the Taylor Swift song "I Can Do It with a Broken Heart" came out, I joked that my version was "I can do it with chronic back pain." Stand for five hours in the floor "seats" of a Taylor Swift concert? Sure! Take a red-eye? Absolutely. Carry a naughty four-year-old out of a store? What other option did I have if he wasn't going to walk? I started running again, just a mile here and there. My husband decided to sign up for a half-marathon near Bar Harbor, Maine, in October, so in a fit of optimism I signed up too. I figured I could always travel with him, pretending that I intended to run the race, and then let him go to the starting line by himself.

But then, slowly, something shifted. There was no one moment. At six months I was still in considerable pain, but by seven months I noticed that it was easing up. My first longer training runs for the half-marathon were slogs. Then, one bright August morning, I took off running down the boardwalk during our annual beach vacation and 9.5 miles later I felt good. Not "good" for a chronic-back-pain patient. Good for my old, healthy self. My antalgic lean disappeared. When we went to Bar Harbor and Acadia over that October weekend, I hiked up Gorham Mountain, and then the next morning I actually ran 13.1 miles, an outcome I could not have imagined during those dark days in January.

I wish there was "one weird trick" I could point to. Trust me, I'd love to be able to bottle my back pain cure and make millions selling it, or at least know I could avail myself of something specific to avoid a relapse. I was doing all the back and leg exercises one was supposed to do as a dutiful physical therapy patient, but I'd been doing those faithfully for a year before my back gave out and wreaked havoc on my nervous system. If they helped, great. They hadn't prevented the problem, nor did my commitment to getting seven-plus hours of sleep at night, walking 10,000 steps a day, eating my vegetables, or all those other pieties we like to believe will prevent bad things from happening to good people.

And so I am left with this conclusion: The key change was time. I did what I could and time did the rest. Time makes good memories fade, but time also makes terrible things less terrible. Time doesn't heal all wounds, but it heals a lot of them.

I truly hate having to be patient. But the good news is that when you believe in big time, then you can afford to be patient. Whatever it is, someday you will be on the other side. One of the wisest bits of parenting advice I have heard is "this too shall pass." Most likely, the kid who demands you sit in his room while he falls asleep at age five is not going to be doing this at age 15. A child who is struggling can, with patience and reminders that he can do hard things, decide that he wants to be a straight-A student—and become one. Time is the secret ingredient, and while there is no guarantee of anything, nothing lasts forever. Whatever the current crisis is will not be the current crisis later. There may be new ones. But if you're patient and supportive, it won't be this one. You do what you can, and wait.

And fundamentally you can believe that time is working with you. Aspen Swett, whose husband is in the military, has moved to numerous new places in her life. "Each move reminds me that it takes *time* to establish community and new routines in a completely different place," she told me. Their biggest move was to Okinawa, Japan, and there was just an incredible amount to learn—"an entirely new culture, time differences to make phone calls back home, driving on the left side of the road, which included buying cars with steering wheels in the proper spot, the pace of my husband's job overseas." In the beginning, "it was overwhelming." But not forever. "Over time, [Okinawa] became this beautiful experience, and it became *home*. We still talk fondly about our experience living overseas." When she wrote me, her husband was on the verge of retiring from the military. "Post-retirement still looks a bit fuzzy, but I'm holding on to the fact that time will be our friend as we step into this completely new season."

Time will be our friend. I love this phrase. When we believe that time is big and hardworking, then we can start to see that it is its own force. It can be on our side. "Not yet" doesn't mean "never." I certainly hold on to this hope whenever I start writing a new book, just as Mary Laura Philpott knew her next project would be out there waiting in the future, on the other side of her creative dormancy. It is hard to see, at the beginning, how anything will take shape. But I know I have done this in the past, and so I can picture the new book on the shelf by the others. I can trust that if I just keep working at it, and keep coming back to it, time will help me see things that I couldn't see before. With patience it will happen, just as sure as a garden blooms, just as sure as a turtle emerges after winter, ready to keep ambling along.

Tactic #1: How to track your time

Knowing where the time goes creates possibilities. If you'd like to try tracking your time, you can use the blank time log following this section, or you can download one in various formats (Excel, PDF, and Google Sheets, all available in 30- and 15-minute versions) from my website, at LauraVanderkam.com. You can also use a time-tracking app, or write down notes in a notebook. I suggest people track time for a week to get the most accurate picture of their lives, but even a few days can be helpful. Make sure to include at least one weekend day when you track. Weekend days are real days too.

My time logs start on Monday morning, but you can start whenever you'd like. If you'd like to use one of my logs and not do a Monday start, you can begin recording in the middle of the spreadsheet and cycle back around to the beginning.

To track your time, write down what you are doing in as much detail as you want. "Work" and "met with manager" are both fine, but one gives you more information to work with later (though the first makes for easier tallying, or creating pie charts). You might think of yourself as an attorney billing your time to different projects, but in this case the projects are things like "driving" or "reading."

Some time is nebulous, and some half-hour blocks are spent on lots of different activities. It's okay. You can write "puttering around the house" or "kids, etc." or "TV/scroll/pick up living room/hangout with Michael." You can also use your judgment on what to record. I don't record every bathroom trip. You can see an example of one of my time logs after this section so you can see how I described blocks of time.

Keep the time log with you. Think about how you might create cues to remember to write down how you're spending your time. Some people find that setting an alarm for three times during the day, at least for the first few days, is helpful. However, if you forget to record what you're doing for a while, just approximate the time later. It doesn't have to be perfect. *It is better to leave a few hours blank than to stop completely.* Most people find that checking in three to four times a day is sufficient, with each check-in taking about a minute.

Weekends can be more challenging to track than weekdays, as life shifts from its usual rhythms. If you are out and about without your log, you can email notes to yourself or send a voice memo and transfer this information to your log later. The good news is that if you start tracking on Monday, you'll have a lot of practice at time tracking by the weekend.

Keep going for 168 hours (one week). If the week you recorded seemed atypical, you might continue recording for a second week, though long-term time trackers soon learn that there is no such thing as a typical week. You can learn something about your life no matter what happens.

After you've recorded your 168 hours, look back over your time log. Here are some prompts to help you reflect.

What do you like most about your schedule? Hopefully something is working well, and you should celebrate whatever that is. If the bright spots in your week involved other people, reach out and let them know.

Look at the major categories of how you spend time. How much time did you spend working? Commuting? Interacting with your family? Sleeping? Exercising? Doing personal care (like showering or putting on makeup)? Doing housework or household administration? Watching television? Reading? How much time is spent in transition? How much time is hard to describe?

Do these numbers reflect how you'd like to spend your time? What would you like to spend more time doing? What would you like to spend less time doing?

What do you think a realistic, ideal week would look like?

What would you like next week to look like? Try thinking through your next week (before you are in it) and scheduling in activities you'd like to spend more time doing. What, logistically, would need to happen for this schedule to become a reality? How will you hold yourself accountable for making these changes?

When you know where the time goes, you can celebrate what is working and make changes that allow you to spend more time on what you value. In general this makes people feel more satisfied with their time, even if life is complex.

BLANK TIME LOG

	MONDAY	TUESDAY	WEDNESDAY
5:00 AM			
5:30			
6:00			
6:30			
7:00			
7:30			
8:00			
8:30			
9:00			
9:30			
10:00			
10:30			
11:00			
11:30			
12:00 PM			
12:30			
1:00			
1:30			
2:00			
2:30			
3:00			
3:30			
4:00			
4:30			
5:00			
5:30			
6:00			
6:30			
7:00			
7:30			
8:00			
8:30			
9:00			
9:30			
10:00			
10:30			
11:00			
11:30			
12:00 AM			
12:30			
1:00			
1:30			
2:00			
2:30			
3:00			
3:30			
4:00			
4:30			

THURSDAY	FRIDAY	SATURDAY	SUNDAY

Here's an example of one of my logs, which I kept during the week of my 2025 Time Tracking Challenge (January 13–19, with a few hours of January 20 tacked on the end).

	MONDAY	TUESDAY	WEDNESDAY
5:00 AM			
5:30	5:40 hear M, up, shower	5:45 up on own	5:45 up on own
6:00	dress, breakfast, hair	doze, up, work	lie in bed, up, shower
6:30	hair, R up, B, ready, drive	coffee/read, R, shower	coffee, R up, eat b-fast
7:00	drive/practice speech	R ready, J, in van, wait, back, S	clean, drive R/van, J, S up
7:30	drive/practice speech	breakfast, chat B (H hiding!), work	work
8:00	stop rest stop, drive	work	make pancakes, boys, sort mail
8:30	drive	work (AQ)	sort mail, in car/drive boys, A
9:00	drive, park, walk around	work (AQ)	drop H, groceries, home
9:30	work/coffee at cafe	(10 min break) work	work
10:00	work/to event	wrap presents, work	work, drive
10:30	work (speech)	work (+ admin: camp, hunt glasses)	haircut
11:00	work (speech)	work (record BB), email	haircut, drive
11:30	work (speech)	work	work/lunch
12:00 PM	work (others talk)	lunch/chat M (phone), work	work (BOBW Patreon)
12:30	to car, drive	work	work (BOBW Patreon)
1:00	drive	mailbox, change, run	work/email/etc.
1:30	stop, get food, drive	run (2), clean up, find glasses	work (BB/G)
2:00	drive	work	work/files, work
2:30	drive	work	work (printing)
3:00	home, unpack, R, work	work, sign R up camp	walk outside, work
3:30	work	R, J measure, work	try make appoint, get A
4:00	walk outside	A, work	back, work
4:30	work	train with virtual trainer	work
5:00	work	laundry, work	work
5:30	work	work	puzzle
6:00	cook dinner	cook dinner/blogs	hangout, H/video, check S
6:30	eat w/kids, help J, drive S	eat w/big kids, hangout	kids ready, to Olive Garden
7:00	home, H dinner, puzzle/H	kids/clean/laundry, read	Olive Garden/A's b-day
7:30	puzzle/H Caillou	watch H play/scroll/email	Olive Garden/A's b-day
8:00	puzzle/H, go get S, home	H bath, hangout H	Olive Garden, home
8:30	Legos w/H	Legos w/H	kids, J printing, etc.
9:00	sit w/H, art w/A, then R	sit w/H, J papers/measure	kids, H ready, stories, out
9:30	art (R,A), kid chats	chat camp w/A, R, A's bath	A down, kids, trash out
10:00	to room (R), read/relax	kids down, scroll/read/relax	trash (w/S), puzzle
10:30	scroll, in bed, sleep	scroll/read/relax, ready bed	puzzle, ready bed
11:00		sleep	in bed/sleep
11:30			
12:00 AM			
12:30			
1:00			
1:30			
2:00			
2:30			
3:00			
3:30			
4:00			
4:30			(up)

THURSDAY	FRIDAY	SATURDAY	SUNDAY
		5:15 up, then sleep	
		sleep	(up)
		up, J, S up for contest, coffee	
0 up, R, shower	6:55 up, R up	boys go, ready, hangout	
R's stuff, H, van, S	coffee, shower, make-up	ready, drive/Beethoven	
ast, B chat, work	R, S, b-fast, talk J, drive	run w/friend	up, shower, H, etc.
ve S, home	drive S, home, little boys	run (5 miles)	breakfast, chat w/M
rk (some boys)	little boys, drive, A	chat, drive, gas/Beethoven	ready, drive to church
rk	drop H, home, coffee, hair	home, breakfast	choir practice
rk	work	shower, kids, dress	choir, texts, etc. prelude
rk	work (MLP/BB)	G gets H, R chat, ready	church
ck, work	work	to car, drive downtown	church
rk (page through logs)	work (VA chat), snack	park, art museum	to Acme, get cake, home
rk (logs)	work	art museum, to car	snack/coffee, puzzle
rk	work	drive, home, lunch	laundry, clean J room w/him
sic practice	work	lunch, drive w/R	clean J room, read
rk, book doc visit, lunch	work (C/BB)	Old Navy shop w/R	clean J room, laundry
rk	work	Starbucks w/R, home	change, run/weights
rk (L/BB)	work, go get girls (R friends)	make gift bags, work	run/weights (2.2), laundry
rk/files, ready, run	girls, home, work/girls	admin, work	work
ghts/run (2.0), clean up	work (+ deal girls)	work, read, 3D print w/A	walk outside, kids
t B/H, H entertain	work (+ deal girls)	3D print w/A, hangout	work/watch H
rk	kids go, walk outside	walk outside, puzzle	work/H, Eagles/TV
rk	work	puzzle	Eagles/TV
k outside, work	work (watching H)	H back, play dinosaurs	Eagles/TV
rk, cook dinner	hangout, start cooking	dinosaurs, help cook	Eagles/TV
rk, eat w/kids, clean	cook, eat dinner w/family	cook, eat family dinner	Eagles - win!
dy, clear car, to choir	eat w/family, clean up	eat, clean up	hangout, etc.
ir rehearsal	piano, hangout	bath for H, watch football/TV	work
ir rehearsal	cake + presents for A	watch football/TV	puzzle
ir rehearsal	kids, read Economist	football/TV, puzzle	ready, H bath
ir, drive home	read Economist	puzzle	out, find M, H, shovel
, B chat, sit w/H	read, H Logoo	puzzle, H milk + stories	shovel w/S
/H, other kids, shut house	H into bed, kids, etc.	sit w/H, he's upset	shovel w/S, in
x/scroll/etc.	A, ready bed	H, ready bed/read	H story, H down
x/scroll/etc.	sleep	sleep	scroll/relax/ready bed
p			sleep
			4:15 up
			(lie in bed)

What I liked most about my schedule: Professionally, I spent a fair amount of time on my favorite kinds of work. I gave a speech to an appreciative and high-energy audience, and I interviewed several fascinating people for my *Before Breakfast* podcast. I led a Zoom meetup for my *Best of Both Worlds* Patreon community and worked on this book. In my personal life, I enjoyed celebrating my fourth child's birthday with a dinner at Olive Garden mid-week. I ran with a friend Saturday morning, sang with my choir, and made it to the art museum. There was time for puzzles and Legos. And watching my favorite TV: the Philadelphia Eagles winning one of their playoff games! I love to be at the games in person a few times a year if I can, but there was a snowstorm on this January Sunday and so I was glad to be cozy inside.

What I want to spend more time doing: I did run four times, but some of these sessions were quite short (two miles). This was partly a function of it being January. The treadmill is boring, but if I'd been more intentional about music or podcast choices, this could have been better. Believe it or not, I would have liked to work more. Because of some less-than-strategic choices, my workdays can get compressed. For instance, on Wednesday I'm not sure I needed to stop at the grocery store at 9:15 a.m. I like my hair salon, but they do offer appointments at times other than 10:30 a.m. on a weekday.

What I want to spend less time doing: My evenings feature a fair amount of "relax/scroll/etc." I didn't have a good book I was reading during the week of this time log. Fortunately, the next week I purchased a good one at an airport bookstore and then wound up reading through that author's entire back catalog, which improved the situation. I might have liked to spend less time shoveling the driveway but at least one of my kids and my husband helped with that.

I love looking at time logs, so if you track your time and would like to share the results with me, feel free to reach out at Laura@lauravanderkam.com.

Tactic #2: How to run a weekly planning session

A regular weekly planning session will help you become the ring-master of your life. Even if life is complex, you can figure out how to make progress toward your goals and keep chaos at bay. Here's how to build such a session into your life.

CHOOSE A REGULAR PLANNING TIME

I tend to plan during the workday on Thursdays or Fridays, look-ing forward to the next Monday-to-Sunday week. The end of the week works well for me, but whatever time you choose, make sure it's a time you can make happen regularly. That way, this planning time will become a habit. If you haven't been doing weekly planning sessions before, the first one might take awhile. But by a few weeks in you should be able to get your marching orders for the week in 30 minutes or less.

I like to plan for my professional life and personal life at the same time, because I am one person, with one life, though it might work better for some people to separate these. If you plan closely with another person, you can aim to coordinate their availability for part of your planning time. For instance, you could sit down with your assistant for 15 minutes as you're planning, or you could call your spouse on your Friday lunch break to check on their schedule and plans and then finish the job on your own afterward. Or you could have a conversation with family members about plans on Thursday night at dinner, and then do your planning on Friday morning.

LOOK AT THE LANDSCAPE

What's going on in the next week? Hopefully you have some sort of calendar where you keep track of your various commitments. If not, go get one! I prefer to keep one master calendar with both work and personal commitments because, again, I am one person with one life, but I know that doesn't work for everyone. If you have both a work and a personal calendar, you'll need to look at them both (ideally at the same time) to reconcile them. To make this system airtight, it's best to get in the habit of putting commitments on your calendar as soon as you learn of them or decide to do them. If you're unsure if you'll do them, put them there with a question mark. If you believe you've forgotten something, go through your email, or any paper notices you've collected, and put what you need to know or might like to do on your calendar. You can also check in more broadly with anyone else who might have desires or obligations that will affect how you spend your time (friends, colleagues, etc.). For instance, perhaps a neighbor mentioned hosting a get-together next weekend and you want to check if that is happening. You don't need to figure out the rest of your life, but you might glance forward a week or two to see if there's anything big coming up you want to be aware of.

MAKE YOURSELF A PRIORITY LIST FOR THE UPCOMING WEEK

You should make this list in three categories: career, relationships, self. Look over your calendar and think about how you'd like to spend your time. What is happening in each of these categories that is most important? Do you need to do anything to prepare for these events or tasks to make sure they go well? Is there anything not yet on your calendar that you would like to see happen? If you think of something, you can create a time on your calendar for it, or simply put it as a task on your priority list, meaning you'll get to it during some open time. Ideally these lists should be short. The act of putting something on the priority list means you intend to do it in the next week.

LOOK AT EVERYTHING ELSE

Study your obligations for the week that don't rise to the level of your top priorities. Do you have a plan and time allotted to tackle everything? Take a moment to think about logistics, both for you and for any family members whose schedules you're managing. Try to spot any potential problems or things that might go wrong. Do you need to move anything or cancel anything? Can you minimize anything that is not a big priority? Do you need help with anything?

MAKE SURE YOU HAVE SOMETHING YOU ARE LOOKING FORWARD TO

Life features a lot of obligations. If the next week looks like all work and no fun, go back and rework the plan until you are genuinely excited about something.

Tactic #3: Build a better workday

In late 2024, I led a group of people through a three-week Better Workday Challenge designed to make their day-to-day working lives better. In general, the people who implemented these strategies wound up enjoying their workdays more.

Here are some questions to help you plan and implement the strategies in your own life over the next few weeks. In the Better Workday Challenge, people asked the planning questions at the start of the week, and then the implementation questions at the end of the week. They learned one strategy each week. You can follow that approach and spread these strategies out over three weeks, or you can do them all at once.

BETTER WORKDAY CHALLENGE STRATEGY #1: SPEND ONE MORE HOUR ON THE WORK YOU LIKE MOST

Planning questions:

- When are you happiest at work? What are you doing? List a few favorite activities.
- What do you like about each of these activities?
- Choose one activity that would make sense to focus on over the next week.
- When did you last do this activity, and for how long?
- How much time would you estimate you spend on this activity each week?

The goal with this strategy is to spend an extra hour on this activity over the next week. Think about today, and the next few work days. When could you make space for this favorite activity on a day like today? Would it make sense to do it all at once, or for 10 to 15 minutes a day over several days?

What would need to happen for you to make time for this favorite activity? Would you need to talk to anyone, shift your schedule, or make logistical arrangements?

What challenges might you face in trying to spend an extra hour on your favorite work?

How could you deal with those challenges?

Make a plan to spend more time on your favorite work. You can put it on your calendar, or to-do list, or talk with whoever will assign you work. Over the course of the work week, try to notice when you are doing this work and take notes about it.

Implementation questions:

- Did you do your favorite work activity? If so, when did you do it?
- What changes did you see in your workday from doing this favorite activity?
- Did you face any challenges in doing this favorite activity— the expected ones or different ones?
- How did you deal with these challenges?
- Will you try to spend more time on this favorite activity in the future? Do you need to modify your plans to make this work?

BETTER WORKDAY CHALLENGE STRATEGY #2: SPEND 15 MINUTES DEEPENING A WORK FRIENDSHIP

Planning questions:

- Who do you enjoy spending time with in your professional life? Think about colleagues or people in your professional network.
- Choose one person to focus on spending time with this week. This could be a colleague or it could be someone in your broader professional network. Who will you choose?

- What do you like about this person?
- When do you normally see this person (either in person or virtually)?
- How much time do you regularly spend together during a workweek?

Think about today, and the next few workdays. When could you spend an extra fifteen minutes with this person on a day like today, or over the next few days? What would you do?

Make a plan to spend more time with this person. You might see each other randomly, but you might also need to make a more structured plan. If you need to take a few minutes to reach out to this person, you could do so now. What is your plan for the next week?

What challenges might prevent you from spending more time with your work friend?

How could you deal with those challenges?

As you go through the week, note when you are spending time with your chosen work friend, or with other work friends or people in your network. Note what you do, and how you feel.

Implementation questions:

- Were you able to spend more time with your work friend? How much time did you spend together?
- What did you do with your time together? What did you talk about?
- How did spending time with your work friend affect your workweek? How did the time together feel?
- Did you face any challenges in spending more time with your work friend—the expected ones or different ones? How did you deal with these challenges?

- Will you try to spend more time with this work friend or other work friends in the future? How might you make that happen?

BETTER WORKDAY CHALLENGE STRATEGY #3: TAKE TWO INTENTIONAL BREAKS EACH DAY

Planning questions:

- Think back to your last work day. Did you take any breaks? What did you do?
- Short breaks can help boost energy, mood, and productivity. What are some ten-minute activities you could do during a workday that would make you feel refreshed? Try to list at least five.
- Think about your schedule today. When could you take short breaks on a day like today? How about over your next few work days? You can choose clock times (2:00 p.m.) or contingent times (after my project-status meeting).
- Look over your schedule for the next few days and choose what you will do on your breaks. What will you do tomorrow? The next day? When will you take these breaks?
- Think through any logistics or planning that will need to happen for you to take these breaks. How will you remind yourself?
- What challenges might you face in trying to take your planned breaks?
- How could you deal with those challenges?

Over the course of the week, note when you take your work breaks, what you do, and how you feel.

Implementation questions:

- Did you take intentional work breaks over the last few days? What did you do? Did any breaks stand out as notable?
- How did taking intentional breaks affect your work days?
- Which kinds of breaks felt most doable? Were any more challenging than others? Were any days or times more challenging than others?
- How did you deal with these challenges?
- Will you continue to take intentional breaks during your work days? Will you need to modify this strategy to make it work for you?

Tactic #4: Embrace your golden hours

During the summer of 2024, I led a group through an Evening Hours Challenge designed to improve people's "golden hours" (the time after work and before bed on weekdays). On average, people who went through this challenge saw their time satisfaction levels rise significantly over the course of the week.

Here are some questions you can ask yourself to make over your own weekday evenings. Try working through the planning questions at the beginning of the week and the implementation questions at the end of the week.

Planning questions:

- What do you like most about your weekday evenings?
- What do you like least about your weekday evenings?
- How did you spend yesterday after work and before bed? If you did not work yesterday, think back to a recent workday,

or you can think about the hours after 5:00 p.m. and before bed in general.

- When do you generally end work for the day? This can be the bulk of the workday; you don't need to include short email or calendar checks.
- When do you generally go to bed on weeknights?
- How much time do you have between the end of work and bed? If you commute, how much time do you have between the end of your commute and bed?

What are some short (30- to 60-minute) activities that you might find enjoyable and that you can do on a weekday evening? You can list activities that you might do on your own or that you might do with other people. These can be activities you do at home or elsewhere. Try to think of at least five, and include some in at least a few of these categories.

From your list, choose three activities you would like to do over the next week. What are those three?

Look at your calendar or think about your regular schedule. When might you be able to do these three things over the next week? You can list clock times (Tuesday at 7:00 p.m.) or contingent times (Tuesday right after dinner).

What challenges might prevent you from implementing these intentions?

How could you deal with these challenges?

Implementation questions:

- Were you able to do any of your evening intentions over the past week? Which ones?
- If you were able to do any of the intentions, what effects did you see in your life?

- What challenges, if any, did you encounter in trying to implement these intentions?
- How did you deal with these challenges?
- If you were not able to do one or more of the intentions, what obstacles prevented you from doing so?
- Do you think these intentions might be doable in the future?

Tactic #5: Go on a "Yes Quest"

Sometimes we get stuck in a default mindset of "no." While it is good to have boundaries, saying yes to things that might be fun or meaningful, even if they're a bit outside our comfort zone, can shake life up in a good way.

To go on your own "Yes Quest" choose a period of time—I chose three weeks—when you say yes more than you usually would. You don't need to say yes to things that sound burdensome, boring, or dangerous. But if you have the time and resources for something, and it sounds interesting, try saying yes.

When you say a yes, keep track of it—the date, the time, the situation—and note any effects on your life. Some yeses might be a waste of time. But others might lead to something more interesting. You just never know. Try to get to at least 10 yeses. If you want to do more, that's great too.

Tactic #6: Take the 8,760 hours perspective

There are 8,760 hours in a year. People often think about the upcoming year at obvious fresh-start times (such as January 1, or the start of an organization's fiscal year). But even if you aren't reading this book in January, I encourage you to spend some time thinking about how you'd like to spend the next year. You can think about what you'd like to see happen both professionally and personally. Knowing where you'd like to go increases the chances that you get there. A few exercises can help.

1. TAKE THE 8,760 HOURS PERSPECTIVE PROFESSIONALLY

Picture yourself 8,760 hours (one year) into the future. You are giving yourself the equivalent of a professional performance review. As you think back on the past year of your working life, you keep saying, "Wow, that was just incredible!" over and over again. In terms of how you spent your time, what made the past year so amazing? Perhaps you might picture yourself marching into your supervisor's office to ask for a promotion and a raise. You know she will say yes because you did X, Y, and Z. What are those things? Or maybe you've kept things as they are at your current job, or you've scaled back modestly, because you've devoted significant time to a side project you're passionate about. What could you have accomplished over a year? Or perhaps you are picturing yourself in a new and more exciting job. What would that be? What would make you pop the champagne corks and throw a celebration? Feel free to dream big. Make a list of your (future) professional accomplishments.

2. TAKE THE 8,760 HOURS PERSPECTIVE PERSONALLY

Picture yourself getting together with an old friend on this day a year in the future. Over lunch, or coffee, or drinks, he says he's never seen you look so happy. What's your secret? You talk about the amazing things you did in your personal life over the past

8,760 hours. You are glowing because you did X, Y, and Z. What are those things?

Make a list of whatever would have you feeling celebratory.

After making lists of what you'd like to be celebrating 8,760 hours from now, think about how much time these things would take. How much time do you think you would need to build into your life to make them happen? Where do you think you could put those hours? Some things are uncertain, but you might be able to estimate. And often these estimations, even if they feel big as you experience them, will seem quite reasonable in the context of 8,760 hours.

A SIMPLE PATH TO TIME ABUNDANCE

I often do "time makeovers" for people—helping them figure out where the time is going now, and what they'd like to change, so they can use the principles in this book and that I teach to spend more time on what matters.

Beth answered a recent call for case studies because she knew I wanted to hear from people with less flexible jobs. "I'm a part-time librarian, so not only do I work fixed hours, I also have fixed 'desk shifts' when I might or might not be able to work on various things depending on how many customers come by," she told me. "My husband and I trade off work days (he is a drafter) so that we can care for our 2-year-old at home with no child care—and we also have two middle schoolers from my first marriage."

Beth reported that she had a good system for prioritizing time during her workday. For instance, she aimed to clear her inbox between customers "on desk" rather than use precious "off desk" time for this task (when she was doing other things for the library).

However, she was looking to be more intentional about the rest of her time, which is not always easy when you are caring for a small child.

She sent me her time log from a recent week, which you can see here (D is the two-year-old).

BETH WEEK 1

	MONDAY	TUESDAY	WEDNESDAY
5:00 AM			
5:30			
6:00		sleep	
6:30	sleep	prep/run	rest/phone scroll
7:00	getting ready	run/bandaging	D/etc.
7:30	laundry, D up	D/breakfast	breakfast
8:00	cook, eat breakfast	breakfast/get ready	getting dressed
8:30	dishes/hair/kids	ready/drive to work	D/chores
9:00	laundry/art/admin	settling in/journal	chores
9:30	play Zelda	chatting/email	chores
10:00	play Zelda	library	Zelda
10:30	laundry/D	core collection	Zelda
11:00	get D ready	desk shift	prep/transition
11:30	outdoor time	desk shift	outside
12:00 PM	lunch	lunch	lunch
12:30	lunch	walk/school research	nap transition
1:00	nap prep/D	reference shift	school application
1:30	admin: schools	desk shift	plumber/chores
2:00	admin: schools	reference shift	plumber/chores
2:30	Jazzercise	desk shift	Woobles/crafts
3:00	Jazzercise	librarian meeting	Jazzercise
3:30	changing and chores	librarian meeting	change/D
4:00	cooking	snack	snack
4:30	D/etc.	Duolingo/packing	crafts/D
5:00	talk R/sweep w/D	desk shift	talk R/chores/D
5:30	cooking	desk shift	make dinner/D/meal plan
6:00	dinner	pack up/drive home	eat dinner
6:30		dinner	birthday party research
7:00	noticing time	put D to bed	news in slow Spanish
7:30	family TV	D/family TV	noticing/family TV
8:00	family TV/crochet	family TV	family time
8:30	reading	crochet/reading	crochet, reading
9:00	getting ready	Duolingo	Duolingo, chatting
9:30	bath	yarn, running bath	talk J
10:00	prep and bed	bath, get ready bed	bath
10:30	sleep	sleep	shower/get ready for bed
11:00			sleep
11:30			
12:00 AM			
12:30			
1:00			
1:30			
2:00			
2:30			
3:00			
3:30			
4:00			
4:30			

THURSDAY	FRIDAY	SATURDAY	SUNDAY
sleep/get ready	get ready, lift		
D, C	lift	sleep, scroll in bed	
breakfast	get ready	scrolling	
get ready	McDonald's w/G	D	scroll in bed
TV, computer time	McDonald's, drive	D/C	get up, make coffee
transition	drive/chat	make scones	Zelda
get ready, leave on bike	meeting	breakfast/prep	Zelda
bike to school	children's desk	eat breakfast	Zelda
bike	children's desk	get ready	get dressed
bike	children's desk	outside	breakfast
lunch	children's desk	transition	transition
D nap, talk J	lunch/chat	go to home goods store	outside
fix button	chat/email	home goods store	D nap prep
Zelda	walk	Zelda	game
Zelda	minor tasks	Zelda	game
Zelda/craft	focused work	Zelda	game
D up	tidying/Duolingo/snack	snack/craft	game
driving to playdate	children's desk	craft	game
playdate	children's desk	D (others play game)	game
playdate	children's desk	D/chores	game
drive/chores	children's desk	D/crochet	game
talk to R/D	going home	D/Duolingo	D
dinner prep	movie night	D/dance party	newspaper/D
eat dinner	movie night	dinner	D
tidying	movie night	news in slow Spanish/tidying	dinner
prep, chores	D	laundry/spelling bee	D
chores/family time	D	research/family time	Duolingo/family time
family TV	family time	family time	family time
family time/reading	family time	crochet/reading	crochet/reading
Duolingo	reading/Duolingo	laundry	tidying
bath		laundry/run bath	getting ready for bed
get ready for bed	bath	bath	bath
sleep	shower/ready for bed	get ready for bed	more getting ready
	sleep	sleep	sleep

I asked Beth what she liked and didn't like. She reported that she liked several things:

"The big picture of my husband and myself both working part time and taking more or less equal responsibility for both breadwinning and child care."

"I am managing 'confetti time' by having books and crochet projects that are ready to grab."

"I think I have a pretty good handle on making sure I am getting high-quality rest. I rarely sit and scroll and call it a break."

"My adolescents wanting to spend time with us after the little one goes to bed is a good problem to have!"

Where did she want to spend more time?

"On big picture things, like advocating for my values."

"Out of the house! The particular week was one where we were more or less snowed in over the weekend, and we're pretty intentional with our time (family movies and board games), but even on nicer weekends I don't always have a big adventure out of the house."

"On 'bigger' craft projects that can't be done during confetti time, like sewing and making photo books."

"Involving my toddler in things that need to get done so that I am not trying to cram everything into the six hours a week when I'm at home with her and she's napping."

"Making my house more organized, more beautiful, and, yes, cleaner. I'm good at batching administrative tasks but less good at batching housework."

I could see that Beth put a lot of thought into her time. For instance, she was often doing Jazzercise during her daughter's naps, and on library days she would squeeze a workout in before her commute. She was using bits of time to learn Spanish. She was taking a mid-day walk when she got a break at work. She was getting to bed at close to the same time most nights. She reported that it had been a fairly stressful week with working on an older child's high school application. She had made time for that, but also spent a fair amount of time playing Zelda because, as she noted, it was her decompression time. I get it!

Ideas to try

I had a few suggestions for Beth. First, just as with work breaks, or the "golden hours" at night, it helps to be intentional with any discretionary time. On the days Beth was caring for her two-year-old, nap time was the equivalent of a mid-day break one might take in an office.

Beth said she wanted to spend more time getting into the flow with longer craft projects. She did bits and pieces here and there (see "family TV/crochet"), but longer stretches are hard to do with a two-year-old underfoot. Since she often did work a weekend day with her job as a librarian (if not in this particular week she tracked), she wanted to spend the remaining day as family time, rather than trading off hobby time with her husband.

So my recommendation was to designate at least one nap time per week as an official "Crafternoon." As soon as her daughter was down, she could dive into a craft project—chosen ahead of time, with the materials all set up—and get at least an hour. If it was a 90-minute to two-hour nap, she could do a workout after that and get both. While an hour a week might not sound like much, as we talked about in chapter 4 with spending an hour extra each week on a favorite kind of work, often it doesn't take much to make life feel different.

Of course, if she was doing crafts during nap time, that raised the question of when she would do chores and home organization. I told her that I thought the bite-size, time-confetti approach she was taking with crafts might be better suited to these projects. A lot of housework and home organization can be done with a two-year-old awake, as long as you have limited expectations. Basically, you can assign yourself five 10-minute "extra" projects per week to address tasks that are more than the usual maintenance, like we talked about in chapter 3 on breaking big projects into smaller steps. You choose one per day, put it on your to-do list, and tackle it during a few free minutes. Maybe that would be when her daughter was happily occupied with a toy, or coloring. Progress might feel slow, but if you do five small projects a week for two months just about any house will look significantly better. Then once the house was more organized and picked up, Beth might begin thinking more seriously about beautification projects and start adding those to the list.

When would she make this list of home projects? She could incorporate this into the regular weekly planning time we talked about in chapter 2. This would also give her an opportunity to think about the "big picture" matter of putting her values into her schedule. A little intention could make this desire much more concrete.

As Beth set her weekly priorities in the categories of career, relationships, and self, she could make a note to add a "values" subcategory, perhaps as part of "relationships." By always listing this as a category, she would nudge herself to put something in it, and to put it on her weekly task list alongside those high school applications and chores.

As for family adventures, she and her older kids could sit down and make a "local bucket list"—a list of some nearby places (including indoor ones for winter) that they'd like to visit. When she did her weekly planning, she could pull one of those adventures off the list and put it into her calendar. Since her teens had helped come up with the list, hopefully they'd be invested in actually doing these adventures when the time came.

Protecting time

Beth considered these ideas. "For crafts, I think you are right that the bottom line is I will need to set aside time and protect it. A whole nap might be unrealistic but I could try either a whole hour once a week (leaving enough nap for a quick workout or a few emails), or maybe one whole nap every other week."

She also liked the idea of making a list of bite-size cleaning tasks and then choosing from the menu of tasks when she did her weekly planning. "I think I will feel better about things that are getting a little dusty if I know their turn to get cleaned will come around eventually. A bonus is that the boys and I do a twice-weekly 'noticing time' that is sort of a 10-minute free clean, and although the idea is for them to notice what needs to be done, in practice they often need suggestions, and now I will have some suggestions ready to go. I already started jotting down some ideas!"

She noted that "I do have a weekly planning time (on Friday afternoons, or sometimes Saturday p.m. if I am working Saturday) and I like the idea to fold values work into that too. I admit I'm not totally sure what I want that to be or look like either—Sending emails to corporations that I patronize?

Identifying local nonprofits? Taking more time to source what we need secondhand when possible to reduce our carbon footprint?" While that was going to require some thought, as she said, "I'm sure I will have more thoughts if I start thinking about it regularly." Over a longer period of time—like 8,760 hours—she might be able to do a lot.

As for planning weekend adventures, "Trying to get the bigger kids to sit down and think about what they would like to do is also a good idea—if I ask them, they just say they don't know!" But they did start a list and had come up with four medium-to-big adventure plans. "Again I think the secret is really just making time to think about it regularly."

She agreed to try these ideas out for a few weeks to see how things went. She tracked another week and sent it back.

BETH WEEK 2

	MONDAY	TUESDAY	WEDNESDAY
5:00 AM			
5:30			
6:00		sleep	
6:30		get ready, R sick	
7:00	sleep	run and stretch	getting ready
7:30	getting ready	breakfast/D	make egg bites
8:00	D	breakfast/R	clean kitchen
8:30	breakfast	get ready for work	eat breakfast
9:00	chores/10 minute clean	biking, settling in	D's bath
9:30	get D ready	children's desk	D
10:00	bike to park	children's desk	chores/make spice mix
10:30	park time	children's desk	chores/10 min clean
11:00	library play time	meeting	outside
11:30	library/bike home	meeting	outside
12:00 PM	make lunch	lunch	lunch
12:30	eat lunch	colleagues/library	kitchen work
1:00	nap prep/start craft	meeting	D nap prep
1:30	craft time	meeting	household admin
2:00	craft time	regroup/library	Jazzercise
2:30	workout	walk	Wooble/craft
3:00	workout/clean up	Duolingo	chores
3:30	D snack	chatting colleagues	Duolingo
4:00	outside	library work	parenting
4:30	finger painting	library work	errands
5:00	screen time/Zelda	library work	errands
5:30	finish dinner, read w/D	closing down	dinner prep
6:00	dinner	transition/bike home	dinner
6:30	transition/tidying	dinner	household
7:00	transition/ready	D	household
7:30	noticing time/family	D/family time	noticing time/family time
8:00	family time	family time	family time
8:30	crochet/reading	crochet/listen to reading	crochet/reading
9:00	crochet/hanging out	financial admin work	reading
9:30	prep bath	run bath/etc.	run bath etc.
10:00	bath	bath/shower	bath
10:30	get ready for bed	get ready	get ready
11:00	sleep	sleep	sleep
11:30			
12:00 AM			
12:30			
1:00			
1:30			
2:00			
2:30			
3:00			
3:30			
4:00			
4:30			

THURSDAY	FRIDAY	SATURDAY	SUNDAY
	sleep		
sleep	prep/workout		
get ready	workout	breakfast	up
D	breakfast	get ready	breakfast
breakfast	get ready for work	get ready	Zelda
get D ready	bike to work	drive, stop at store	Zelda
bike ride	advise colleague	settling in/library	dishes
community meeting	meeting	library work	chores/D/newspaper
meeting	emails/program prep	desk	hanging out
bike home	library work	desk	rest
D	library work	small tasks	get ready
make lunch and dinner	lunch	lunch	D
eat lunch, D	library work	children's desk	transition
D, nap prep	library work	children's desk	walk
coffee/admin	walk	library work	laundry
household admin	library work	library work	laundry
household admin	library work	walk	crochet/finish show
Zelda	snack/Duolingo	circulation training	snack/reset
Zelda	children's desk	children's desk	10 min clean, ready
cleaning/D helps	children's desk	children's desk	get D ready
D's snack	children's desk	children's desk	travel for Super Bowl
outside time	children's desk	children's desk	Super Bowl party
D, TV, resetting	pack up, bike home	drive home, settle in	Super Bowl party
dinner prep w/D	transition	dinner	Super Bowl party
dinner	dinner	D	Super Bowl party
transition	put D to bed	get D ready for bed	Super Bowl party
resetting	TV and crochet	get D ready for bed	Super Bowl party
read/family time	TV and crochet	movie	Super Bowl party
family time	talk J and crochet	movie	Super Bowl party
crochet/read to R	run bath	movie	drive home
Duolingo, run bath	bath	movie	drive/put D to bed
bath	early sleep	movie	
get ready for bed		fold laundry	
sleep		talk about movie	
		bath	
		get ready for bed	
		sleep	

Sometimes changes aren't immediately obvious on time logs, but Beth's "Crafternoon" was. Her Monday time diary entry shows a bit over an hour devoted to a craft project during nap time. Beth happily reported that "I have only missed one week of craft hour!" This was true even though her daughter was no longer napping consistently. The family was still enforcing a rest hour and the good news is that around the time children stop napping for good, they often do start preschool a few mornings a week, which might open up some space in the future. "I finished my first project, an apron for my husband, and started my next project, a ruffled apron for myself." She had supplies for her next project and had plans to visit a fabric store with a coworker. "I've been really good about protecting the time and not letting chores or scrolling impinge on it."

She reported that she had started coming up with values-related tasks during her planning time, then doing them. "Sometimes it is something formal, like calling my congress-woman or starting a monthly contribution to my local food bank, and sometimes it's something less formal, like planting wildflower seeds that a coworker harvested for me from his gar-den (values: supporting the environment in the form of insect life and community building). Most weeks I have a home admin hour and that's when I try to steal some values time."

Beth was also "still chugging along with confetti time chores and making adventures happen. Sometimes I do a chore that I had planned and sometimes I just do something that's bother-ing me that day, but the important thing is to pick something that I can FINISH. I could spend all day futzing around trying to pick up! But I do a task or two and move on mentally."

As for adventures, Beth said, "I haven't even needed my list of fun activities that I made because things keep coming up—having our board game group over, taking my middle kid to a STEM showcase, a coworker friend gathering up a group for cheese 'n' chocolate at the Melting Pot. But I have it in case there's a week that seems dull!"

These tweaks were helping her leisure and family time feel more intentional. "This experiment has been really fun and helpful for me and seeing myself make slow but consistent progress on my projects is really satisfying," she noted. Slow progress is still progress, and each day and each week is a chance to try again.

ACKNOWLEDGMENTS

I love writing books. It's my favorite sort of work, and I am grateful for the chance to get to write another one. Thank you to Merry Sun and the team at Norton for taking a chance on this project, helping to shape it, and seeing it through to publication. Thank you to Laura Mucha, Caroline Adams, Meredith McGinnis, Erin Sinesky Lovett, Rebecca Springer, Julia Druskin, Steve Attardo, Daniel Lagin, and Jane Cavolina for their contributions.

I am also grateful to Laurie Abkemeier of DeFiore and Company for helping me craft the proposal and for representing this project. A big thank you to Cal Newport for introducing us.

Big Time would not exist without all the readers who participated in my Time Tracking Challenge, the Better Workday Challenge, and the Evening Hours Challenge. I am grateful for everyone's generosity with their time. I also appreciate Jessica Webb's continuing expert guidance on setting up surveys, and her concise and insightful analysis of the results.

Thank you to everyone who agreed to be interviewed for this book. Your willingness to share your stories will help other people spend their time better too.

Thanks to the members of the Writers Strategy Group, my mastermind friends, and to Sarah Hart-Unger for their professional feedback and support. I am also grateful for administrative and strategic support from Kim Cardillo, November Lee, and Jenell Stewart.

And of course I'm grateful to my family—Michael, Jasper, Sam, Ruth, Alex, and Henry—for giving me such a wonderful circus to manage. May we always choose the bigger life.

NOTES

CHAPTER 1: REWRITE YOUR STORY

13   **the most commonly used noun:** "The Commonest Noun in English Is 'Time,' According to Oxford Dictionaries," Oxford Dictionaries press release, March 31, 2012, https://www.pr.com/press-release/401950.

13   **The average number of hours worked:** Charlie Giattino, Esteban Ortiz-Ospina, and Max Roser, "Working Hours," OurWorldinData.org, 2020, https://ourworldindata.org/working-hours. While some of the decline in average hours is attributable to the fact that women are more likely to be in the workforce now, and women tend to work fewer hours than men, before modern labor standards, hours in male-dominated fields such as manufacturing and industrial work tended to be quite long. Estimates of lifetime leisure hours for men tend to have risen substantially (for one discussion, see Robert Whaples, "Hours of Work in US History," Economic History Association, August 14, 2001, https://eh.net/encyclopedia/hours-of-work-in-u-s-history).

13   **in 2024 the average American spent:** "Table 1. Time Spent in Primary Activities and Percent of the Civilian Population Engaging in Each Activity, Averages per Day by Sex, 2024 Annual Averages," American Time Use Survey, US Bureau of Labor Statistics, June 26, 2025, https://www.bls.gov/news.release/atus.t01.htm.

18   **I used a time-satisfaction scale:** Laura Vanderkam, *Tranquility by Tuesday: 9 Ways to Calm the Chaos and Make Time for What Matters* (Portfolio, 2022), 251–53.

CHAPTER 2: BECOME THE RINGMASTER

50   **One study found that when people:** Colin West, Cassie Mogilner, and Sanford E. DeVoe, "Happiness from Treating the Weekend Like a Vacation," *Social Psychological and Personality Science* 12, no. 3 (2020): 346–56, doi: 10.1177/1948550620916080.

CHAPTER 3: DREAM BIG, PLAN SMALL

72   **reasons suggested by a fascinating study:** Cassie Mogilner, Zoë Chance, and Michael I. Norton, "Giving Time Gives You Time," *Psychological Science* 23, no. 10 (2012): 1233–38; doi: 10.1177/0956797612442551.

CHAPTER 4: STOP WISHING TIME AWAY

74   **In 2023, 54 percent of employed respondents:** Megan Brenan, "Americans Largely Satisfied with Their Personal Life," Gallup, February 23, 2023, https://news.gallup.com/poll/470888/americans-largely-satisfied-personal -life.aspx.

74   **an eyebrow-raising Gallup poll:** Frank Newport, "In U.S., Most Would Still Work Even if They Won Millions," Gallup, August 14, 2013, https://news .gallup.com/poll/163973/work-even-won-millions.aspx.

74   **study asked people to report their moods:** Daniel Kahneman, Alan B. Krueger, David A. Schkade, Norbert Schwarz, and Arthur A. Stone, "A Survey Method for Characterizing Daily Life Experience: The Day Reconstruction Method," *Science* 306, no. 5702 (2004): 1776–80. For a chart of ranked activities, see Daniel Kahneman and Alan B. Krueger, "Developments in the Measurement of Subjective Well-Being," *Journal of Economic Perspectives* 20, no. 1 (2006): 3–24.

75   **The average workweek in March 2025:** U.S. Bureau of Labor Statistics, "Average Weekly Hours of All Employees, Total Private," September 5, 2025, https://fred.stlouisfed.org/series/AWHAETP.

77   **things like feeling a sense of competence:** Richard M. Ryan and Edward L. Deci, "Self-Determination Theory and the Facilitation of Intrinsic Motivation, Social Development, and Well-Being," *American Psychologist* 55, no. 1 (January 2000): 68–78, doi: 10.1037//0003-066x.55.1.68.

85   **Having close friendships at work:** Alok Patel and Stephanie Plowman, "The Increasing Importance of a Best Friend at Work," Gallup, August 16, 2022, https://www.gallup.com/workplace/397058/increasing-importance-best -friend-work.aspx.

89   **One meta-analysis of 22 studies:** Patricia Albulescu, Irina Macsinga, Andrei

Rusu, Coralia Sulea, Alexandra Bodnaru, and Bogdan Tudor Tulbure, "'Give Me a Break!' A Systematic Review and Meta-Analysis on the Efficacy of Micro-Breaks for Increasing Well-Being and Performance," *PLoS ONE* 17, no. 8 (2022), doi: 10.1371/journal.pone.0272460.

CHAPTER 5: EMBRACE YOUR GOLDEN HOURS

104 **data from the American Time Use Survey:** Nathan Yau, "A Day in the Life," Flowing Data, December 15, 2015, https://flowingdata.com/2015/12/15/a-day-in-the-life-of-americans.

CHAPTER 6: BE OPEN TO SERENDIPITY

123 **Karen Schneider, a writer for The Muse:** Karen Schneider, "I Said Yes to Everything for a Year and Here's What Happened," The Muse, June 19, 2020.

128 **political scientists Anna Helgøy and Ana Catalano Weeks:** Anna Helgøy and Ana Catalano Weeks, "Crowded Out: The Influence of Mental Load Priming on Intentions to Participate in Public Life," *British Journal of Political Science* 55 (2025): e29, doi: 10.1017/S0007123424000826.

CHAPTER 7: THINK 8,760 HOURS, NOT 24

144 **The Social Security Administration publishes actuarial tables:** Social Security Administration, Actuarial Life Table, http://ssa.gov/oact/STATS/table4c6 .html. These are 2021 mortality rates, as used in the 2024 Trustees Report.

149 **Consider Aleksandr Lyubishchev:** See @greatrandomizer, October 17, 2024, https://www.threads.net/@greatrandomizer/post/DBN9wI2NVhZ /he-tracked-every-minute-of-his-life-for-56-years-and-developed-a-produc tivity-sy.

156 **"He who reconciles with reality":** See @greatrandomizer, October 17, 2024.

CHAPTER 8: BE PATIENT

159 **"a precious gift to the world":** Katie Hafner, "Worry Much? You'll Relate to Mary Laura Philpott's Book," review of Mary Laura Philpott, *Bomb Shelter*, *Washington Post*, April 11, 2022.

160 **it would be as "genius":** Judith Warner, "Is It Possible to Body-Block Our Loved Ones from Pain? Alas, No," review of Mary Laura Philpott, *Bomb Shelter*, *New York Times*, April 5, 2022.

162 **According to Guinness World Records:** Adam Milward, "Introducing Jonathan, the World's Oldest Animal on Land at 187 Years Old," Guin-

ness World Records, February 27, 2019, https://www.guinnessworldrecords
.com/news/2019/2/introducing-jonathan-the-worlds-oldest-animal-on-land
-561882.

163 **people who rated their marriages as "unhappy":** Linda J. Waite et al., "Does
Divorce Make People Happy? Findings from a Study of Unhappy Marriages,"
Institute for American Values, 2002, https://www.healthymarriageinfo.org/
wp-content/uploads/2018/05/UnhappyMarriages.pdf.

166 **anticipation accounts for the bulk of the happiness:** Jeroen Nawijn,
Miquelle A. Marchand, Ruut Veenhoven, and Ad J. Vingerhoets, "Vacationers
Happier, but Most not Happier After a Holiday," *Applied Research in Quality
of Life* 5, no. 1 (2010): 35–47. doi: 10.1007/s11482-009-9091-9.